8/2004

$34

W9-CCD-105

8/12/04

Uncoupling Convention

Bending Psychoanalysis Book Series

Jack Drescher, M.D., Series Editor

Volume 1
Uncoupling Convention: Psychoanalytic Approaches to Same-Sex Couples and Families
Ann D'Ercole and Jack Drescher, editors

Volume 2
Who's That Girl? Who's That Boy?
Lynne Layton

First Published 1999 →

Volume 3
→ *Notes from the Margins: The Gay Analyst's Subjectivity in the Treatment Setting*
Eric Sherman

Are out in August 2005

Uncoupling Convention

Psychoanalytic Approaches to Same-Sex Couples and Families

cso

Edited by
Ann D'Ercole and Jack Drescher

 THE ANALYTIC PRESS

2004   Hillsdale, NJ   London

Published by The Analytic Press, Inc.
101 West Street, Hillsdale, NJ 07642
www.analyticpress.com

Typeset in Palatino 11/13 by Michael Saridis Design
Index by Writers Anonymous, Inc., Phoenix, AZ

Library of Congress Cataloging-in-Publication Data

Uncoupling convention : psychoanalytic approaches to same-sex couples and families /
    edited by Ann D'Ercole and Jack Drescher.
        p. cm.
    Includes bibliographical references and index.
    ISBN 0-88163-238-4
        1. Psychoanalysis and homosexuality. 2. Gays—Mental health. 3. Lesbians—Mental
health. 4. Gays—Mental health services. 5. Psychotherapy. I. D'Ercole, Ann. II. Drescher,
Jack, 1951-

    RC451.4.G39U536 2003
    616.89'17'08664—dc21   2003056093

Printed in the United States of America
10 9 8 7 6 5 4 3 2 1

This book is dedicated to
the memory of our dear colleague and friend
Adria Schwartz.

Contents

Acknowledgments

I am indebted to each of my patients and students, for they have contributed immeasurably to my thinking through and formulating this project. I thank all the contributors for their creative efforts that made this work possible. I particularly wish to thank my community of colleagues at the New York University Postdoctoral Program in Psychotherapy and Psychoanalysis, whose innovative and integrative ideas are woven throughout the book.

I wish to express my love and appreciation to my family. I am grateful to Tony, Marci, and their amazing children, Andrew and Kaley; and to David, Amy, and their fabulous daughter, Frida, and to Laura and Helen. Their generous patience and their love have been my beacon. It is with pride and gratitude that I add a special thanks to Laura for adding her unique sociologist's perspective to this volume. To Linda goes my deepest gratitude for her inspiration, encouragement, sustaining humor, and love.

I thank my coeditor Jack Drescher for his wise and energetic collaboration and for his concise critiques that moved the project along a faster track. A special thanks to John Kerr, who launched the project and, along with Paul Stepansky, kept it moving and the staff at the Analytic Press, particularly Meredith Freedman for her editorial assistance.

— Ann D'Ercole

❋ ❋ ❋

I want to thank all the authors in this volume for their creative, thoughtful, and original contributions. I also want to thank Ann D'Ercole for getting me to participate in a project that added greatly to my own clinical knowledge.

I am indebted to Paul Stepansky for inviting me to edit the *Bending Psychoanalysis* book series. Thanks to John Kerr, whose unmatched editorial capabilities created a standard I can only hope to emulate. Thanks to all the staff at TAP for their unfailing commitment to producing and promoting great books.

I wish to acknowledge the early pioneering contributions of the late Stuart Nichols, Judd Marmor, Stephen Mitchell, John Fryer, Frank Rundle, and CA Tripp. They are all deeply missed, although the spirit of their lives and their work lives on.

I am grateful to my family for their love and support during the illness and after the passing of my father, Mayer Drescher.

I can never thank Nishan enough for being the constant source of inspiration in my life.

— Jack Drescher

Contributors

J. P. Cheuvront, Psy.D. is a candidate at the Institute for the Psychoanalytic Study Of Subjectivity (IPSS), New York City; clinical supervisor, Yeshiva University's doctoral programs in psychology; and was the 1997 recipient of the Jeffrey Sage Memorial Award for Excellence in Clinical Psychology.

Ann D'Ercole, Ph.D. (editor) is Faculty, Supervisor, and Clinical Associate Professor at the New York University Postdoctoral Program in Psychotherapy and Psychoanalysis; editor, *Journal of Gay and Lesbian Psychotherapy* and coeditor, *Psychotherapy with Gay Men and Lesbians: Contemporary Dynamic Approaches* (2003).

Jack Drescher, M.D. (editor) is Fellow, Training and Supervising Analyst, William Alanson White Psychoanalytic Institute and Chair, Committee on GLB Concerns of the American Psychiatric Association. Dr. Drescher is editor-in-chief, *Journal of Gay and Lesbian Psychotherapy* and author of *Psychoanalytic Therapy and the Gay Man* (1998, The Analytic Press).

Deborah F. Glazer, Ph.D. is Faculty and Supervisor, Psychoanalytic Institute of the Postgraduate Center for Mental Health and the Psychoanalytic Psychotherapy Study Center (PPSC) and coeditor, *Gay & Lesbian Parenting* (2001).

Suzanne Iasenza, Ph.D. is Associate Professor of Counseling, John Jay College of the City University of New York, and is Faculty, The Institute for Contemporary Psychotherapy and the Institute for Human Identity. She is coeditor (with Dr. Glassgold) of *Lesbians and Psychoanalysis: Revolutions in Theory and Practice* (1995).

Judy Levitz, Ph.D., NCPsyA is the founding director of the Psychoanalytic Psychotherapy Study Center in New York City where she also teaches and supervises.

Barbra Zuck Locker Ph.D., ABPP is a Supervisor, New York University Postdoctoral Program in Psychotherapy and Psychoanalysis, New York City.

Laura Mamo, Ph.D. is an Assistant Professor of sociology at the University of Maryland, College Park. Her forthcoming book is tentatively titled: *Queering Reproduction: Lesbians, Biomedicine, and Reproductive Technologies*.

The late Adria Schwartz, Ph.D. is the author of *Sexual Subjects: Lesbians, Gender and Psychoanalysis* (1998).

Melanie Suchet, Ph.D. is a candidate at New York University Postdoctoral Program in Psychotherapy and Psychoanalysis.

Introduction

Ann D'Ercole and Jack Drescher

There is an old song that claims "love and marriage go together like a horse and carriage." It is no small irony, however, that the buggy is an outmoded form of transportation and that the heterosexual divorce rate in the United States hovers at 50 percent. With the blending of families of divorce, both heterosexual and gay, traditional marriage arrangements are becoming increasingly passé as well. As Adria Schwartz notes in her contribution in this volume, "Ozzie and Harriet Are Dead."

How one responds to their deaths may vary. For political conservatives, reports of their death seem premature. For them, such cultural shifts are a spur to stem the tides of change. For others, change seems inevitable. They see these changes as providing new opportunities to understand the conventional underpinnings of the couple and the family. As psychoanalytic writers, editors, and clinicians, we believe it is an opportunity and a challenge to understand the impact of a changing culture on the lives of our patients.

The late Stephen Mitchell (1998) called marriage a hazardous arrangement, an undertaking not for the faint of heart. The contributors to this volume ask the reader to imagine the stressors in maintaining committed relationships where the possibility of legal marriage is foreclosed. Or to consider the impact on families in which both parents often do not and cannot have a legal relationship with the child they are raising These realities are the subtext in this collection of contemporary psychoanalytic essays of gay and lesbian couples and families. The couples and families discussed here are not in legal, conventional marriages. And although their relationships may resist being defined, categorized, and classified, they also resist being excluded and marginalized.

The contributors to this volume also resist being categorized into one school of psychoanalytic or psychotherapeutic thought. They nevertheless share a willingness to work with and accept the lived lives of gay people. Both in theory and practice, the contributors affirm and sometimes redefine what it means to be a member of a gay/lesbian couple or family. Toward that end, the contributors reasoning draws from two significant cultural movements of the twentieth century: psychoanalysis and the struggle for gay and lesbian civil rights.

There are certainly special challenges for the psychoanalytic clinician working with patients who present for treatment as having troubled relationships. Consider Freud's ill-fated treatment of the American psychiatrist, Horace Frink. Freud encouraged Frink to divorce his wife and to marry a woman who was Frink's own former patient. Freud simultaneously urged this woman to marry Frink. Frink's divorce and remarriage, possibly motivated by Freud's attempt to secure financial assistance for the psychoanalytic movement from the new wife, culminated in a worsening of Frink's manic-depressive symptoms and a subsequent divorce from the rich wife Freud had chosen for him. Whatever the first wife's presumed defects, she had apparently provided a stabilizing influence on Frink (Kramer, 1997). Although not all treatments produce such extreme results, such outcomes support the position that a psychoanalytic process can be intrinsically meddlesome. In fact, the analyst is usually invited in to interfere. As he often preached what he himself did not practice, Freud cautioned other analysts not to accept the invitation:

> Young and eager psycho-analysts will no doubt be tempted to bring their own individuality freely into the discussion, in

order to carry the patient along with them and lift him over the barriers of his own narrow personality. It might be expected that it would be quite allowable and indeed useful, with a view to overcoming the patient's existing resistances, for the doctor to afford him a glimpse of his own mental defects and conflicts and, by giving him intimate information about his own life, enable him to put himself on an equal footing. One confidence deserves another, and anyone who demands intimacy from someone else must be prepared to give it in return. . . . I have no hesitation, therefore, in condemning this kind of technique as incorrect [1912, pp. 21–28, 117–118].

Despite its attempts to reduce the potential for therapeutic mischief, psychoanalytic neutrality remains an idealized and elusive goal. The developmental theory with which the analyst works will inevitably valorize some aspects of a patient's relationship while devaluing others. Consider the rather common analytic tendency to use hierarchical, developmental models to contextualize a patient's relationship. The analyst may regard a patient's partner or spouse, for example, as meeting infantile desires or needs. If those needs or desires are believed to be the result of psychological regressions or fixations, the analyst might try to get the patient to see the futility of trying to gratify them in a relationship. Although this analytic approach to treatment is certainly not confined to gay couples, historian Martin Duberman's (1991) experience in psychoanalysis illustrates the principles contained within this analytic attitude:

From the first [my analyst] Weintraupt advised me to give up the relationship with Larry. Until I did, he warned, any real progress in therapy would prove impossible. The drama of our interpsychic struggle, Weintraupt insisted, had become a stand-in for the more basic intrapsychic conflict I was unwilling to engage — the conflict between my neurotic homosexual acting out and my underlying healthy impulse toward a heterosexual union. I resisted — not so much Weintraupt's theories, as his insistence on a total break with Larry. I accepted the need, but could not summon the will. I spent therapy hour after therapy hour arguing my inability to give up the satisfactions of the relationship — neurotic and occasional though they might be, and though my future happiness might well hang on their surrender. I resisted so hard and long that Weintraupt finally gave me an ultimatum: either give up Larry or give up therapy [p. 33].

Duberman's analyst, in threatening to terminate the treatment, followed a standard psychoanalytic prescription of an earlier era, one which encouraged patients to change or abandon their homosexuality (Ovesey, 1969). The clinical technique was based on a theoretical model, translated into a widespread clinical practice, that tried to force patients to choose between their symptoms (the wish to have a same-sex relationship) and their health (the wish to maintain the tie to the analyst). Mitchell (1981) calls this a directive-suggestive approach deliberately designed to manipulate patients, ostensibly for their own good. In fact, this deviation from analytic neutrality was further sanctioned by the introduction of the psychoanalytic concept of parameters (Eissler, 1953). As Laplanche and Pontalis (1973) put it "Even the most orthodox [psychoanalysts], however, may be led in particular cases — especially cases involving anxiety in children, the psychoses and certain perversions — to waive the rule of complete neutrality on the grounds of its being neither desirable nor practicable" (p. 272).

In retrospect, the actions of analytic forbears appear outrageous, perhaps even unethical. As in Freud's treatment of Frick, sometimes an analyst's own needs, broadly defined as countertransference, will interfere with the ability to see what makes a relationship work for a particular patient. Because an analyst's opinions can have a critical impact on their patients' relationships, analysts need to ask themselves the criteria that they themselves use to determine appropriate standards of relating. And upon what basis do they favor one type of relationship over another — scientific studies, theoretical models, clinical experience, or strategies — that have worked for the therapist? How do therapists transmit relational values to patients, and to each other in training and in supervision? In clinical practice, this usually occurs in how analysts decide which of the patient's feelings and behaviors to interpret. Which feelings toward a patient's partner are to be regarded as emotionally authentic and which will the analyst interpret as defensive? Complicating matters further, given what we know of patients' wishes to transferentially please their analysts, how can we know if our interpretations are accurate or simply reflect false-self compliance (Winnicott, 1960) from the patient? Here the challenge for the analyst lies between being elevated to a position of power and authority over the patient while simultaneously remaining very human (Hoffman, 1998).

Traditional psychoanalytic narratives of development, attachment, and relatedness have drawn on heterosexual perspectives. This volume's clinical focus on gay and lesbian couples and families incorporates perspectives from cultural, feminist, gay and lesbian, and queer studies. Queer theorists in particular have illustrated how the concepts of gender and sexuality are routinely informed by unproven heterosexist assumptions – both conscious and unconscious – within the culture (Butler, 1990, 1991, 1995; Harding, 1998; Drescher, D'Ercole, and Schoenberg, 2003), This holds true not only in many of the theoretical assumptions of scientific inquiry, but in virtually every aspect of daily life (Drescher, 1998). Inarticulated assumptions about gender and sexual identity inform cultural conceptions of who is and who is not a person (Butler, 2003). They also raise questions about what is and what is not a couple or family.

Historically, to be a "homosexual" was to suffer from a mental disorder, to be a criminal, to be invisible, to be counted as not fully human. Living one's life as a "homosexual" was thought to invite a life of loneliness. Vestiges of these belief systems remain today. Although the gay man walking with a baby carriage discovers that everybody smiles at him, what would people think and how would they behave if they knew that not only did he have no wife, his partner is another man? Thus, another important question for clinicians treating gay and lesbian patients is how do the cultural meanings of homosexuality intersect with cultural constructions of the couple and the family? In what ways, successfully or otherwise, do lesbian and gay couples and families strive to deal with a cultural dissonance generated by their very identities?

In the first essay, "Ozzie and Harriet Are Dead: New Family Narratives in a Postmodern World," the late Adria Schwartz provides an insider's glimpse of gay and lesbian couples and families. She describes the emotional complexities of parenting in a world of diverse familial configurations where fewer than 25 percent of Americans live within the nuclear television family of the 1950s. Schwartz notes that gay families in the United States are estimated to include 14 million children. She points out that the nature of caretaking figures cannot be taken for granted in today's world of genetic mothers, gestational mothers, adoptive mothers, and men as mothers.

In asking psychoanalytic clinicians and theoreticians to recognize more accurately families as they exist today, Schwartz simultaneously exhorts them to recognize the limitations of the classical oedipal triangle and that "triangles" have become obsolete. New family constellations, Schwartz argues, necessitate a rethinking of traditional notions of identification and internalization as well as theories regarding internal representations and self states. What she calls "new family narratives" suggest that multiple internal parental relations change over time in tune with changing developmental needs, changing family dynamics, and a changing culture.

In "Gender 'In-Difference': Gender Development in Lesbian-Parented Families," Melanie Suchet also takes on the question of what counts as a family. Suchet argues that the construction and dynamics of dichotomized, hierarchically organized gender identities is restrictive and oppressive, both intrapsychically and culturally. Because they do not serve the children of same-sex couples well, she radically proposes giving up what she calls the false truth of gender, that is abandoning traditional notions of gender differences altogether. She exhorts parents to be open and flexible, to hold onto the multiple realities of gender and to live in them and in the spaces in between. This would allow for the construction of a different form of gender subjectivity in children and their parents.

J. P. Cheuvront also addresses the question of what is a couple. In "Couples, Imagined," he describes the critical role of imagination in the lives of couples. Regardless of how couples are imagined or gendered, they come to therapy because of their unhappiness, anxiety, and conflict. Cheuvront suggests that a couples therapist has an opportunity to listen to patients' experience and imagine equally fulfilling ways of living that may differ from the way the couple currently lives. In contrast to Suchet, he notes that influences from society cannot be eliminated. Nor, for that matter, can influences from the life of the therapist be kept out of the clinical setting. From Cheuvront's intersubjective perspective, it is important to be aware of personal influences, to inspect both the therapist's and patient's presumptions about couples. If they are willing to hear and be educated by patients' subjectivities, therapists can enhance their capacity for identifying and entertaining new ways for patients to conceptualize, assess, and potentially feel satisfied with their chosen relationships, regardless of how those relationships are configured or gendered.

How do contrasting cultural constructions of homosexuality and family life make themselves felt as same-sex couples traverse different life stages? Although several contributors take up this point, two in particular — D'Ercole and Levitz — address the impact of underlying, unconscious antihomosexual feelings and how they can be obscured by more superficial conflicts. In "The Interplay of Difference and Shame: A Lesbian Couple in Treatment," Ann D'Ercole cautions analysts to be aware of how a gay patient's shame and self-hatred can emerge in the clinical setting. She uses clinical material to demonstrate the intense interplay between difference and shame in a lesbian couple, noting that underlying feelings of shame can be obscured by other issues a couple may bring into treatment. D'Ercole illustrates how, through the metaphor of feelings of "difference," feelings of shame about one's sexuality can remain unacknowledged and unnoticed.

Judy Levitz, in "'Is This Normal?' Uncovering the Role of Homophobia in the Treatment of a Lesbian Couple," sees a couple as a new family. When the honeymoon is over, each member of the couple's internal families are inevitably activated. As in the larger culture, these internal families are characterized by both conscious and unconscious antihomosexual attitudes — powerful forces whose inner existence needs to be acknowledged. In a creative mixing of theoretical approaches, Levitz

offers a survival kit to keep powerful transferences and enactments minimized for the couple, the therapist, and the treatment itself.

In "Teasing Apart Gender, Object Choice, and Motherhood
in Lesbian Relationships," Deborah Glazer addresses not only
the question of what is a couple, but also the intersection of
the cultural constructs of a lesbian identity with the wish to
mother. Like D'Ercole, she, too, sees the clinical presentation
of "difference" as a complex subject warranting closer scrutiny. She notes that for some lesbians, the need to come to
terms with what it means to be a woman who is not a wife, to
be a women who loves women rather than men, and to be a
woman who may not automatically desire to mother is critical. Glazer notes how issues such as competition between two
lesbian mothers can point to underlying issues of intimacy,
authenticity, and responsibility that have an inevitable impact
upon family dynamics. She further illustrates how when the
child of lesbian parents begins to experience antihomosexual
biases, this may activate earlier, traumatic experiences of the
mothers' own coming out.

As D'Ercole's, Levitz's and Glazer's chapters illustrate, the
question of how an individual integrates stigmatized and val-
orized identities is an important one for psychoanalytic theory
and clinical practice. For most gay men and lesbians however,
this is experienced as more of a practical matter than an academic question. For many gay men and lesbians, the more
pressing issue is home economics and domesticity rather than
queer theory.

In contrast to the psychoanalytic perspectives of the other
contributors to the volume, Laura Mamo offers a perspective on
"The Lesbian 'Great American Sperm Hunt': A Sociological
Analysis of Selecting Donors and Constructing Relatedness."
As a sociologist, Mamo steps away from the notion of desire and
asks us to look directly at what people do and the meanings
they attach to those behaviors. Using in-depth interviews to
gather data, she describes the experience of women who are in
the process of making their families. She raises the issue of how
medical technology shapes behavior. She explains how the
social experience of "being" a lesbian and wanting to conceive

becomes a biomedical experience that subsequently shapes the reproductive experiences of lesbians. Using the construct of "affinity ties," Mamo goes on to explain how the lesbian family's choice of a sperm donor constructs an idea of relatedness — linking the biological and social to create real or perceived social connections.

In "Passion, Play, and Erotic Potential Space in Lesbian Relationships," Suzanne Iasenza wants to talk about sex — really. She offers a relational frame in the treatment of a lesbian couple that permits an exploration of the multiple meanings of erotic dreams and transference, as well as acknowledging and exploring the therapist's countertransference. For Iasenza, sexual feelings, fantasies, wishes, and fears are understood as transference–countertransference, fundamentally and irreducibly interactive. Her lesbian-affirmative therapeutic approach helps the therapist as well as the couple in treatment to cocreate the erotic potential space within which couples may recover or discover the passions and play in their erotic life.

Sex is one practical matter in the life of a couple. So is money. In "One Plus One Equals One: Money Matters in Same-Sex Relationships," Barbra Zuck Locker suggests that for those willing to take a chance on love, there is a concomitant willingness to take a chance on money. Locker sees money, and the way couples — straight or gay — handle their finances, as an unexplored bastion of secrecy. She believes the way people deal with money reflects a great deal about their characters, their histories, and the influences of the cultures and subcultures in which they live. Money can create an imbalance in relationships that may present as a resistance to or defense against further intimacy. Her lively clinical case material illustrates how financial problems often mask other problems in a relationship.

These essays are offered to the reader as the opening of a psychoanalytic discourse that looks at gay and lesbian couples and families in the context of their lives as lived. We believe that this dialogue will not only prove vital to expanding existing psychoanalytic theory, but also that it is central to meeting the need for affirmative psychoanalytic work with lesbian and gay couples and families. This will be good not only for psychoanalysis, but also for the patients who come to us for help as well. As

Adrienne Rich (1991) puts it:

It will not be simple, it will not be long
It will take little time, it will take all your thought
It will take all your heart, it will take all your breath
It will be short, it will not be simple.

References

Butler, J. (1990), *Gender Trouble*. New York: Routledge.
——— (1991), Imitation and gender insubordination. In: *Inside/Out: Lesbian Theories, Gay Theories*, ed. D. Fuss. New York: Routledge, pp. 13–31.
——— (1995), Melancholy gender — refused identification. *Psychoanal. Dial.*, 5:165–180.
——— (2003), Violence, mourning, politics. *Studies Gender & Sexual.*, 4:9–37.
Drescher, J. (1998), *Psychoanalytic Therapy and the Gay Man*. Hillsdale, NJ: The Analytic Press.
——— D'Ercole, A. & Schoenberg, E. (2003), *Psychotherapy with Gay Men and Lesbians: Contemporary Dynamic Approaches*. New York: Harrington Park Press.
Duberman, M. (1991), *Cures: A Gay Man's Odyssey*. New York: Dutton.
Eissler, K. (1953), The effect of the structure of the ego on psychoanalytic technique. *J. Amer. Psychoanal. Assn.*, 1:104–143.
Freud, S. (1912), Recommendations to physicians practicing psycho-analysis. *Standard Edition*, 12:109–120. London: Hogarth Press, 1958.
Harding, J. (1998), *Sex Acts: Practices of Femininity and Masculinity*. London: Sage Publications.
Hoffman, I. (1998), *Ritual and Spontaneity in the Psychoanalytic Process: A Dialectical-Constructivist View*. Hillsdale, NJ: The Analytic Press.
Kramer, P. (1997), *Should You Leave? A Psychiatrist Explores Intimacy and Autonomy—and the Nature of Advice*. New York: Scribner.

Laplanche, J. & Pontalis, J. B. (1973), *The Language of Psychoanalysis*. New York: W. W. Norton.

Mitchell, S. A. (1981), The psychoanalytic treatment of homosexuality: Some technical considerations. *Internat. Rev. Psycho-Anal.*, 8:63–80.

———— (1998), Reply to commentary. *Psychoanal. Dial.*, 8:561–572.

Ovesey, L. (1969), *Homosexuality and Pseudohomosexuality*. New York: Science House.

Rich, A. (1991), Final notations. In: *An Atlas of the Difficult World: Poems 1988–1991*. New York: W. W. Norton.

Winnicott, D. W. (1960), Ego distortion in terms of true and false self. In: *The Maturational Processes and the Facilitating Environment*. New York: International Universities Press, 1965, pp. 140–152.

1

Ozzie and Harriet Are Dead
New Family Narratives in a Postmodern World

Adria E. Schwartz

According to the 2000 Census, less than one-quarter of the households in the United States resemble Ozzie and Harriet's television family of the 1950s, also known as the "traditional" psychoanalytic family: mother, father, and their biological children (Schmitt, 2001). Today we cohabit or "partner," live in single-parent homes, extended families, blended stepfamilies. Among these configurations, gay and lesbian families are proliferating exponentially. Psychoanalytic theory has yet to take these families seriously. Lesbian and gay families especially are rarely written about, and we have yet to acknowledge fully the implications of their proliferation.

Our children are growing up in a postmodern world, and that is our world as well. It is a world increasingly based on resistance to identity, a questioning of the dichotomous binary categories of male and female, homo- and heterosexuality, that constrain sexual practice and gender performance (Rose, 1986). The postmodern world recognizes the social construction of gender and its interface with the body (Goldner, 1991). The postmodern family, a family formed often by alternate forms of conception (AFC) as well as adoption, formal and informal, impels us to reconceive our notions of what it is to be a mother or father and to question whether the gendering of parenthood is relevant to our understanding of development at all.

13

This essay was inspired partly by a recent period in which I attended a variety of Bar Mitzvah ceremonies in the New York area. The Bar and Bat Mitzvah rituals mark the Jewish child's entrance into the world of adult religious responsibility. It is an appropriate starting point, in that these rituals, occurring as they did in the late 1990s, also mark the coming of age of one of the earliest cohorts of children born to openly proclaimed lesbian- and gay-identified and alternatively conceived families of origin in the United States.

Lesbians have always raised children, of course. But those families consisted mostly of woman who had birthed children within the heterosexual families that they later left to form new ones. There have always been "Boston families," if I might expand on Faderman's (1993) concept of a "Boston Marriage," families such as Anna Freud's and Dorothy Burlingham's in which women raised children together without having a defined sexual identity (Peters, 1985). But these "Bar Mitzvahs," these children of whom I speak, were birthed and adopted into same-sex parented families, or single-parent families, by choice.

Attending these ceremonies crystallized, in a moving and palpable form, questions with which I have been grappling for the past 15 years: Who and what is a mother? Need the construct be gendered? Can a child have two mothers? What issues might arise between these mothers? And what of the fathers, or the sperm donors, known or unknown? Let me take you on quick tour of these families:

- Barry was adopted from South America at the age of 14 months by his moms, both of whom had been married to men before begin-ning their relationship. Rachel is the legal adoptive mom, Michaela is a full coparent. Barry refers to Rachel as Mom and to Michaela by her nickname, Mikki.
- Gabriel had been the product of one of the first legal two-parent same-sex adoptions in the state of New York. Also present at Gabriel's ceremony and given an *aliyah* (honor at the reading of the Torah) was his biological father, a gay-identified man who had donated his sperm and agreed to acknowledge paternity. Known as the donor, but not as dad, Chris sees Gabriel once or twice a year for a weekend visit.

* Eli's two moms separated after two decades of partnership. Eli spends almost equal time with each of his moms, although his biological mom assumes the "bottom line" accountability of the residential parent. Each of the two mothers has a new partner. In this family, the sperm donor is unknown. All of the extended families of both parents, East Coast and West, attended this Bar Mitzvah including the lesbian-identified sister of one of the parents who is also raising a son. Hence, one of Eli's first cousins is also the son of a lesbian mom.
* Howard was adopted at birth by his bisexually-identified mom and was raised for the most part in a single-parent household. But Howard's "real family" consists of his mom, her old boyfriend Robert, and two additional female parenting figures, very much present in his life. With a lesser degree of consciousness and pre-sence, there are also the shadow bio-parents of his birth.
* The final Bar Mitzvah of this particular year was Brian, born of alternative insemination through an unknown donor, to a hetero-sexually-identified woman who raised him as a single parent for the first seven years of his life until she married Marvin. Brian is very attached to Marvin and thinks of him as his dad, rather than the sperm donor.

How are these families discussed in training? How does psychoanalysis discuss families with adopted children, multicultural families, a family where one parent is the legal or socially sanctioned parent and the other is not? How are primal fantasies discussed in which the parents were of the same sex, where the putative father was referred to as a donor, known or unknown? When I think about the people and families that I actually see in my office, I find little or no mention of them in the majority of formal meetings I attend or papers that I read (Patterson, 2001).

New Families: New Narratives
Given the varied configurations that characterize more and more of today's families — including many same-sex families — a reconsideration of psychoanalytic theory and practice is long past due. The so-called traditional family may still exist: Harriet may still be in the kitchen baking her cookies; hardworking,

dependable Ozzie may be off to the office; and they may spend the after-dinner hour chuckling over the antics of Ricky and David, the fun-loving, harmlessly mischievous kids they have conceived and raised together. But these days, in the United States, Ozzie and Harriet are the nontraditional family. Aside from the number of children being raised in heterosexually-identified families that have experienced divorce, living in blended stepfamilies, or in single-parent households, there are an estimated 6 to 10 million lesbian and gay parents in the United States. These gay- and lesbian-identified parents are the fathers and mothers of an estimated 14 million children throughout the country, including those conceived within a heterosexual union (Buell, 2001).

Psychoanalytic theory in its origins was radical in many ways, most especially for the naming of infantile sexuality and the elucidation of what came to be known and later challenged by feminists, gender and queer theorists, and postmodernists, among others, as the theory of psychosexual development. Freud struggled brilliantly, but unsuccessfully, within the confines of his theory, to explain the differences between the sexes, processes of identity formation and gendering, and sexual orientation in its broadest form, all of which relied ultimately for resolution, on the Oedipus complex.

Postmodern culture is much more at ease with ambiguity and a continuum of genders, sexualities, and familial arrangements. Relational theories in particular have the capacity to address today's postmodern family.

These theories take a significant step away from a drive-centered focus of the child subject to an appreciation of the subjectivity of the parenting ones (Benjamin, 1988). They recognize that internalized object relations are a function of the child in multiple relations to the significant others around her. A child's internal representations are of her relational patterns, cumulative interactive histories with significant others: a series of repetitive interactive events that are mutually derived and subjectively constructed (Stern, 1989). These representations are a function of both objective events and subjective experiences. A relational perspective allows for the possibility of a system of caretaking figures whose gender, sexual orientation, or biological relation to their offspring cannot or should not be taken for granted. Thus, reproductive technology has taken the Nature out of Mother in a way that motherhood is no longer bound to simple biology (Schwartz, 1994). There are genetic mothers, gestational mothers, adoptive mothers. Is there a "real mother" when, for example, one woman donates her ova to another who becomes pregnant through in vitro fertilization? If that gestational mother gives the child up for adoption, or raises it with another woman, who is the "real" mother? Is there a real mother? If biology no longer allows for a simple definition of Mother, can gender? Can a man be a mother? The answers are neither simple nor obvious.

The reconstruction of motherhood implies the reconstruction of families as well.[1] Mothering no longer rests within the confines of a heterosexual matrix, nor is it bounded by a gender-binaried foundation.[2] Many children today have a number of people in their lives who nurture and care for them and with whom they have consistent and repeated interactions in a form that they will internalize as maternal parental representations. The deconstruction of gendered motherhood allows one to envision a new parenting subject within relational theories. This is a more conditional conception of parenting that transcends gender and assumes mutual subjectivity (Benjamin, 1988).

Stern (1985, 1989), Beebe (1986), Bowlby (1988), and others tried to integrate infant observation with psychoanalytic theories of attachment and development. Their work is implicitly dependent on the assumption of a single caretaking (female) mother. As yet this work does not refer to the actual families in which our children live: children who have multiple caretakers, multiple moms of both genders. Thus, the use of gendered parental terms to identify either biologically based kinship or

---

[1] For an extensive discussion of a new family discourse, see Weston (1991).

[2] The use of gendered parent terms to distinguish either biologically-based kinship or roles within families is becoming increasingly less relevant in new family narratives. The terms "mother" or "father" are obviously problematic in same-sex parented families but are also becoming less relevant in single-parent families in which children may be mothered by multiple caretakers within and without the extended family, and the single mom may be the "father" as well.

roles within families seems less relevant in new family narratives. In fact, the true meaning and relevance of the terms "mother" or "father" are nominally problematic in same-sex parented families.

Triangles Obsolete
The oedipal triangle lies at the cusp of classical psychoanalytic theory as it formulated psychosexual, moral, and ego development. Boys were said to compete with and ultimately identify with their fathers and their fathers' gender role, and little girls abandon their mothers as primary love objects in search of the inevitably superior phallus (Freud, 1925). The successful resolution of the oedipal phase renders one at peace with one's gender, heterosexually inclined, and emotionally ready to procreate.

The oedipal conflict traces the vicissitudes of desire and identification. Others see it as reifying heterosexuality (Butler, 1990). From the latter perspective, oedipal dynamics are more about power than about sexuality; more about the power of gender privilege implicit in jealousy and gender envy. Triangular dynamics, the swirling eddy of jealousies and alliances, can operate in a much more complicated field of emotions.

I have previously suggested (Schwartz, 1986) the term "triangulation" as an alternative to discussions of the Oedipal stage, in recognition of the latter's lack of applicability in same-sex and single-parent families. In addition, Oedipal language underestimates the effects of triangulation vis-à-vis gender and embodied sexuality in the period referred to as preoedipal. I have come to question, however, whether triangulation adequately represents the internalized relations of children at all. Given the absent biological parent in same-sex parented families, the primary constellation consists of a minimum of four people rather than three. In lesbian-parented families, the absent biological parent is the sperm donor. In gay male–parented families, it is the biological mother. In heterosexual families with an infertile parent, it may be either. In these and in adoptive families, the biological parents are a shadow carrying the child's genetic history. The shadow is difficult to see. Put a spotlight on it and it disappears, yet its presence lingers behind evanescently.

What is there of significant psychological import in the shadow of the absent parent(s)? The child of a friend used to refer to her sperm donor as the "donut." The sperm donor as shadow member of a family carries with it the ambiguity of a donut, where in looking at the hole it is unclear whether there is or is not something missing. There are, after all, all different kinds of donuts.

When the notion of a sperm donor is introduced into the creation of a family, this promotes a paradoxical construction and deconstruction of the father. He both does and does not exist. He is both real and imagined (Ehrensaft, 2000, p. 391). How the "donut" is introduced, and how it is carried internally and externally within a same-sex parented family, may vary for different members of the family. Without more detailed clinical or empirical evidence, one cannot say that the sperm donor is necessarily a significant figure in a young child's early life (Crespi, 2001). Yet it is reasonable to assume that conscious and unconscious fantasies most likely exist around a sperm donor or biological father, whether known or unknown, acknowledged as whole object (bio father) or part object (donated sperm) (Ehrensaft, 2000).[3]

In fact, the fantasies around alternative forms of conception may resemble those families with adopted children. Adopted children have at least three or four parents: two birth parents and one or two adoptive parent(s). Like birth and biological parents in adoptive families, these biological parents, sperm donors, gestational and genetic moms in same-sex parented families can exist as psychic shadows. One important distinction between adopted and AFC children is that issues of the child's abandonment and rejection are not intrinsic in the case of children conceived of reproductive technologies. When such issues exist, they may present in a subtle and less clearly articulated way, such as fantasies of remuneration for the sale of sperm or ova.

---

[3] In my clinical and supervisory practice, these fantasies (if they exist) do not appear to be problematic for young children. This finding, or rather the lack thereof, was corroborated by April Martin (1993), in *The Lesbian and Gay Parenting Handbook: Creating and Raising Our Families*, one of the first and still central references on gay and lesbian parenting.

There are shadow figures that arise with adoptions as well. These will depend on the child's ability to integrate his or her biological birth history, known and fantasized, with the current internalized and actual familial constellation. For example, a young adopted boy, whose treatment I supervised, had night fears about the "shadow people" who sometimes haunted him at night. He feared they might come take him away. Concretely, the "shadow people" were a function of actual shadows reflected off his Venetian blinds. Treatment revealed, however, that his fantasy reflected both his wish and his fears that he might be reclaimed by his biological parents.

Adopted children have to deal with their shadow families of origin and express their uncertainties about them in the issues of abandonment or rejection. Adoption challenges their identities and may evoke feelings of displacement, being lost or in an unexplained exile from a nebulous somewhere. Adopted children often contend with feeling "different." They might feel different from their adoptive families physically, in temperament, or intellectual goodness of fit. But this may be the case in any family. Freud (1909) noted that most latency-aged children develop fantasies about having been adopted and that they are heir to another different set of imagined superior parents. This family romance is an expression of every child's ambivalence toward his or her parents and a harkening back to an earlier time in childhood when parents were more firmly idealized (Brinich, 1990).

Adoption into a gay- or lesbian-identified family might, at first glance, be seen as an additional stressor for a child already having to deal with the trauma of putative rejection. In same-sex parented families, many with cross-cultural, transracial adoptions, that "difference" is starkly apparent.

Same-sex couples and single parents–to-be are often conflicted, unsure as to whether they want to or "should" add to the potential stress of any child growing up by introducing yet another "difference." Although the most comprehensive data pertaining to children raised in same-sex parented families do not deal specifically with adoption. Research shows (Patterson, 2001) that being raised in a same-sex-parented family has no harmful effects on the child (American Academy of Pediatrics, 2000).

Gay- and lesbian-identified parents, however, even more than heterosexually identified adoptive parents, have to prove themselves in a way that biological parents do not (Glazer, 1998). They must analyze and be prepared to defend their readiness and motivation to parent. For gays, lesbians, and same-sex couples, this process can exacerbate internalized homophobia.

The "Real" Mom Problem

Directly stated, can a child have two "real" mothers? Children, having no preconceptions as to how families are structured, accept their own family as the norm until they realize otherwise. Children in preschool settings, for instance, will often meet the news that a classmate has two moms with, "Wow, you're lucky. I wish I had two moms!" (Wendy McKenna, 2001, personal communication). In my experience, clinical and personal, the "real mom" issue is one between the parents, not between parents and child. This issue is illustrative of the ways in which one can begin to think meaningfully about new family narratives, and how, as clinicians and theoreticians, we might be better able to listen and understand.

The issue of the real mother is particularly salient in families composed of two lesbian-identified mothers, where one is the "bio" mother and the other not. There are some situations in which both mothers can claim to be biological mothers (in which one partner donates her egg to the other, and the child is conceived through in vitro fertilization), but the number of lesbian couples doing this is still too small to draw any meaningful clinical impressions about the relationships between these parents. In families where "real mom" difficulties arise, one parent gives birth to, and most likely nurses a child, leaving the other parent to contend with feelings of envy, exclusion, and insecurity about her baby or toddler's attachment. When both women have an intense desire to conceive, or one woman is unable to conceive, these issues may be compounded even further.

In my clinical experience with these couples, I have come to question the effect of birthing and nursing on the bonds between mothers and child, that is, between birth mom and child, coparent and child, and the bond between the mothers themselves. In work with lesbian couples, the nonnursing mom may complain of feeling excluded from the primary dyad. She may complain of having the baby, toddler, or three- or four-year-old reject them at times when certain forms of comforting were required. She may complain of never really being able to "get in" in the same way that the birthing and nursing mom can.

In my work with Vicki these issues became apparent. She and Margaret were a couple whose struggles span two issues that may arise in same-sex parented families: competition between moms and the exacerbation of that competition when one mom is the birthing and nursing parent. Vicki was an artist who worked both at home and as a consultant outside the home. Margaret was a part-time academic, again working both at home and outside.

Margaret used alternative insemination through an anonymous donor to conceive their son. She had promised Vicki they would share parenting equally, just as they had shared in selecting the criteria for donor selection, the insemination process, and Josh's last name. After Josh was born, Vicki wanted very much to use a breast pump to facilitate a sympathetic lactation in order to share both the nursing responsibilities and the nursing experience. Margaret balked, and became adamant in her disapproval of the project. Despite her intellectual belief in the project, emotionally she was not able to relinquish the primary maternal field or share it equally with Vicki. She "confessed" that "deep down" she believed that a child can have only one "real" mother, and that was going to be her. Vicki, according to Margaret, had the brilliant career, one with which she could never successfully compete, despite her own marked accomplishments. This essential motherhood was the one thing Margaret could claim as her own.

Vicki capitulated to Margaret's wishes reluctantly but without much resistance. She had always struggled with feeling that she was not a "real girl." In fact, some lesbians who have grown up feeling "not female like mother" have a much more difficult time envisaging themselves carrying and birthing a baby. Their feeling of not being a "real girl" is based on a de-identification with mother, often begun during the rapprochement stage. It continues on throughout childhood and is again evoked with intensity during adolescence. This de-identification develops partially as a function of perceived gender privilege in a household, coupled with a depressed or narcissistic mother where maternal rejection and or neglect is often confused with gender (Schwartz, 1986, 1998).

Consequently, Vicki did not fight more effectively for equal participation in the nursing process because of her unconscious conviction that she was unable to do so. How could she be a "real mom" if she was not a "real girl?"[4] As Josh grew older, Vicki faded into the background whenever she was asked to by either Margaret or her son. Because both moms sometimes worked outside the home, Josh quickly learned that he could exercise control over what must have appeared to him as their random comings and goings. He did so by strongly exercising his preferences for which mom was to do what and when. Given Margaret's desire to be the preferred mother and Vicki's insecurities about her ability to be a mother at all, Josh controlled both moms in a way that led Vicki to become increasingly estranged and critical of Margaret's parenting while Margaret grew increasingly angry and resentful and withholding of affection. The relationships between mothers and son became more skewed by Josh's frequent and strong preferences for Mommy Margaret over Mommy Vicki: at bedtime, bath time, on the way to preschool. Vicki was profoundly upset at Josh's apparent preference for her partner at crucial moments. But how could it be otherwise when she so often colluded with the asymmetry?

In heterosexual couples, it is not uncommon for fathers to feel excluded from the mother–infant dyad. A father might experience deep feelings of abandonment by his spouse or exclusion from the dyad. This may evoke rivalrous rage and feelings of worthlessness (Donna Bassin, personal communication). In some heterosexually identified families, moms and dads are less likely to compete with each other's parental roles. Traditionally, the months of earliest infancy were ceded to mothers, especially nursing moms, with fathers not really moving closer until the child becomes a toddler (Armelini, 2001). That is now changing

---

[4] For an interesting case of a lesbian struggling with infertility coupled with her feelings of not being a "real woman" see Bassin (2001).

as fathers become more involved earlier. Competition between heterosexual parents continues to be mitigated by gender roles, however, in which it is expected that moms and dads will have different kinds of relationships with their children.

In same-sex couples, gender roles create different kinds of dilemmas. For example, when both partners in a lesbian couple wish to birth a child, there is a question as to who will do so first. Aside from practical considerations such as age or whose career might be better able to incorporate a pregnancy and maternity leave, these decisions involve identifications that can facilitate or impede the progress toward pregnancy (Glazer, 2001).

Vicki wanted very much to birth a baby. Margaret, however, went first, ostensibly because she was already in her mid-30s, five or six years older than Vicki. It was also the case that Vicki couldn't imagine actually being pregnant and bringing a child to term. She had recurrent dreams of hairy and deformed babies long before she ever seriously contemplated becoming a mother. At the time, these dreams seemed to represent both her own sense of deformity and monstrousness, herself as the abject object of her parents' physical and emotional abuse, and in part, an expression of her internalized homophobia (Butler, 1995; Herek, 1998). In fact, when Vicki first came into treatment, despite being a prominent "out" artist she claimed to actually hate lesbians. She assumed that there was something essentially wrong with them, a developmental arrest perhaps, in which they deviated from a normal heterosexual course. She expressed no desire to change her sexuality, but rather seemed resigned to her defect and had an unconscious presumption that she would ultimately be punished, most likely by dying from AIDS.

Vicki's previously noted conviction that she was "not a real girl," her de-identification with her mother-as-female, coupled with her internalized homophobia, left her — as it does with many gay men and lesbians — uncertain about her identity and eroded her confidence as a mother. As Vicki's analysis progressed, however, she announced playfully, after seeing the film *Junior*, "If Arnold Schwarzenegger can become pregnant, I guess I can, too." She decided to choose the same unknown donor as Margaret, so that Josh would have a biologically related sibling. This practice has become increasingly more common as lesbian and gay parents seek to create larger families and seek to bind children biologically in a world that still holds chosen families suspect.

Vicki, after a devastating miscarriage, birthed a son who nurses voraciously, smiles constantly, and whose love is a constant reassurance to Vicki that she can be a "real mom" and a good mom at that. Nonetheless, Vicki still struggles with feelings of illegitimacy. She lives in constant dread that something awful will befall one or both of her children by way of illness, accident, or malevolence. She worried about this with Josh, but the fears have increased exponentially with the birth of her second son. Her analysis has revealed that Vicki's fears are due to lingering doubts that she and Margaret, as lesbians, are truly entitled to the happy family that they seem to have created. In Vicki and Margaret's family, their partnership was essentially sound, loving, and aspiring toward a fundamental noncompetitiveness and equality. Their difficulties arose out of their insecurities about mothering, in Vicki's case about competence and legitimacy, in Margaret's about its ability to be authentically shared.

Issues of asymmetry in early attachment and, consequently, of jealousy, envy, exclusion, and competition might arise more frequently in lesbian couples in which there is one biological and nursing mom than in lesbian couples where an infant is bottle-fed. Competition between lesbian moms can begin here and extend through middle and late childhood, with the nonbiological mom feeling always a little less than, not quite equal to, the biological mom in the child's eyes. This fear, of course, may be exacerbated by the attitudes toward the nonbiological mother's extended family or surrounding culture.[5] How the two mothers handle this asymmetry, should it exist, depends in part on the internalized maternal representations that each of the mothers carry on both the conscious and unconscious ground of their partnership.

---

[5] Let us not forget that that without benefit of a second-parent adoption, the coparent has no standing in health or educational institutions — those institutions most crucial to her child's well-being.

Conclusion

When psychoanalytic clinicians and theoreticians recognize the limitations of the oedipal triangle they may more accurately recognize families as they exist today. These families have forced a rethinking of our notions of identification and internalization as well as our notions of internal representations and self states (Bromberg, 1998).

Each parenting person forms a unique set of attachments and internalized relational representations that changes and develops over time (Loewald, 1973). Each parent is a parent in her particularity. Difference need not be read hierarchically. There is "no real mom," no "real father" because the very concept of the real parent is in itself problematic.

New family narratives reveal multiple internal parental relations changing over time in tune with changing developmental needs, changing family dynamics, and a changing culture. Triangles have become obsolete. Today's families live in a queer and diverse universe of new shapes, new dynamics, and complexity.[6]

References

American Academy of Pediatrics (2002), Policy statement on co-parent or second-parent adoptions, same-sex parents. *Pediatrics*, 109:341–344.

Armelini, M. (2001), The father as function, environment and object. In: *Squiggles and Spaces: Revisiting the Work of D. W. Winnicott Vol. 2*, ed. M. Bertolini, A. Giannakoulas & M. Hernandes. London: Whurr Publishers, pp. 37–46.

Bassin, D. (2001), A barrenness of body and theory: An analysis of infertility. *Studies Gender & Sexual.*, 2:63-82.

Beebe, B. (1986), Mother-infant mutual influence and pre-cursors of self-object representations. In: *Empirical Studies of*

---

[6] Queer: "All people who are attracted to people of the same sex or whose bodies or sexual desires do not fit the dominant standard of gender and/or sexuality." See Beemayne and Eliason (1996, p. 5). Diversity refers to the postmodern critique of universality as it appears in all theory and concomitantly to our increasing sensitivity to difference.

Psychoanalytic Theories, Vol. 2., ed. J. Masling. Hillsdale, NJ: The Analytic Press, pp. 27–48.

Beemayne, B. & Eliason, M. (1996), *Queer Studies: A Lesbian, Gay, Bisexual and Transgender Anthology.* New York: New York University Press.

Benjamin, J. (1988), *The Bonds of Love: Psychoanalysis, Feminism and the Problem of Domination.* New York: Pantheon.

Bowlby, J. (1988), *A Secure Base: Clinical Applications of Attachment Theory.* London: Routledge.

Brinich, P. (1990), Adoption from the inside out: A psychoanalytic perspective. In: *The Psychology of Adoption,* ed. D. Brodzinsky & M. Schecter. New York: Oxford University Press, pp. 42–61.

Bromberg, P. (1998), *Standing in the Spaces: Essays on Clinical Process, Trauma, and Dissociation.* Hillsdale, NJ: The Analytic Press.

Buell, C. (2001), Legal issues affecting alternative families: A therapist's primer. *J. Gay & Lesbian Psychother.,* 4(3/4):75–90.

Butler, J. (1990), *Gender Trouble and the Subversion of Identity.* New York: Routledge.

———— (1995), Melancholy gender-refused identification. *Psychoanal. Dial.,* 5:165–180.

Crespi, L. (2001), And baby makes three: A dynamic look at development and conflict in lesbian families. *J. Gay & Lesbian Psychotherapy,* 4(3/4):7–29.

Dimen, M. (1991), Deconstructing difference: Gender splitting and transitional space. *Psychoanal. Dial.,* 1:335–353.

Ehrensaft, D. (2000), Alternatives to the stork: Fatherhood fantasies in alternative insemination families. *Studies Gender & Sexual.,* 1:371–399.

Faderman, L. (1993), Nineteenth-century Boston marriage as a possible lesson for today. In: *Boston Marriages: Romantic But Asexual Relationships Among Contemporary Lesbians,* ed. E. Rothblum & K. Brehony. Amherst: University of Massachusetts Press.

Freud, S. (1909), Family romances. *Standard Edition,* 9:235–241. London: Hogarth Press, 1959.

———— (1925), Some psychical consequences of the anatomical distinction between the sexes. *Standard Edition,* 19:248–258. London: Hogarth Press, 1961.

Glazer, D. (1998), Lesbian mothers: A foot in two worlds. *Psychoanal. & Psychother.*, 16:142–151.

——— (2001), Lesbian motherhood: Restorative choice or developmental imperative? *J. Gay & Lesbian Psychother.*, 4(3/4):31–43.

Goldner, V. (1991), Toward a critical relational theory of gender. *Psychoanal. Dial.*, 1:249–272.

Herek, G. (1998), Stigma and sexual orientation: Understanding prejudice against lesbians, gay men, and bisexuals. *Society for the Psychological Study of Lesbian and Gay Issues.* Thousand Oaks, CA: Sage.

Loewald, H. (1973), *On Internalization: Papers on Psychoanalysis.* New Haven, CT: Yale University Press, 1980, pp. 69–86.

Martin, A. (1993), *The Lesbian and Gay Parenting Handbook: Creating and Raising our Families.* New York: Harper Perennial.

Mitchell, S. (1988), *Relational Concepts in Psychoanalysis.* Cambridge, MA: Harvard University Press.

Patterson, C. (2001), Families of the lesbian baby boom: Maternal mental health and child adjustment. *J. Gay & Lesbian Psychother.*, 4(3/4): 91–107.

Peters, U. H. (1985), *Anna Freud: A Life Dedicated to Children.* New York: Schoken Books.

Rose, J. (1986), *Sexuality in the Field of Vision.* London: Verso.

Schmitt, E. (2001), For first time, nuclear families drop below 25% of households. *The New York Times*, May 15.

Schwartz, A. (1986), Some notes on the development of female gender role identity. In: *Psychoanalysis and Women: Contemporary Reappraisals*, ed. J. Alpert. Hillsdale, NJ: The Analytic Press, 1994, pp. 57–79.

——— (1994), Taking the nature out of mother. In: *Representations of Motherhood*, ed. D. Bassin, M. Honey & M. Kaplan. New Haven, CT: Yale University Press, pp. 240–255.

——— (1998), *Sexual Subjects: Lesbians, Gender and Psychoanalysis.* New York: Routledge.

Stern, D. (1985), *The Interpersonal World of the Infant.* New York: Basic Books.

———— (1989), The representations of relational patterns: Developmental considerations. In: *Relational Disturbances in Early Childhood*, ed. A. Sameroff & R. Emde. New York: Basic Books.

Weston, K. (1991), *Families We Choose: Lesbians, Gays, Kinship*. New York: Columbia University Press.

2

Gender "In-Difference"
Gender Development in Lesbian-Parented Families

Melanie Suchet

One day, while accompanying my two-and-a-half-year-old daughter to the potty, she exclaimed with delight: "I have a penis and a vagina." Oh, I said, surprised, somewhat bemused but trying to take her seriously. "Oh yes," she said, laughing with glee, "do you want to see?" She thereby pulled down her pants, pointed to her genital area and, moving from front to back, she said "That hole is the penis, there's the vagina, and there's the bum." Then with head held up high, she insisted that she would pee standing up through her penis. A few minutes later she sat down to complete her business, while flashes of Freud, Kubie, Aron, Benjamin, Dimen, Goldner, Harris, and Layton went whirling through my mind. I wondered what it meant for her at this particular nexus in her development to fantasize a penis without giving up her vagina. A month or two before she had told me, quite adamantly, that she was not a girl, she was a boy and a girl. These particular incidents raise several interesting questions regarding the interplay of body and gender. How has meaning been inscribed on the body? What does being a boy *and* a girl offer that being a girl alone does not? Is it really gender she is referring to? What does she understand of my own relationship to my body and gender? How does she, a child in a lesbian-parented family, come to play with and understand her body and her gendered sense of self? Most important, are sex and gender always the most salient and primary lenses through which we construct difference and understand development?

My intention in this chapter is to push the envelope regarding our psychoanalytic thinking of gender. I have chosen the planned lesbian family as a medium through which we can explore and rethink our notions of gender development. In lesbian families, gender is often used, experienced, and performed differently from traditional gender-based parental structures. In particular, gender is not the primary source of difference. Hence any differences or inequalities that exist between the couple are not necessarily tied to gender. Moreover, if gender is removed from the foreground of difference, as the primary and supraordinate organizer of psychic life, it is possible that other critical variables will come into focus, such as differences in power, agency, and connectedness. As Coates (1997) so eloquently commented, "we have reached a point in gender studies where we need to focus on the function of gender in particular contexts, not on gender itself" (p. 50). This chapter will explore how development can be understood differently in a context of gender "indifference," rather than gender as the source of all difference.

Bodies: To Have or Not Have, Is This the Question?
Psychoanalysis was founded on the dominant role of the body in shaping and constructing mental life. Relational theory has moved toward reclaiming the body from classical theory (Harris, 1996, 1998; Dimen, 1998). From this perspective, the body is viewed and understood as constructed and emergent in an intersubjective matrix. It is constituted in social and historical contexts. Between mother and child, one can imagine the coconstruction of meaning that bodies come to express. As Harris (1996) so clearly articulated, the body ego is shaped by the holding, looking, touching encounter of the mother/other. The child's body is laden with meaning for the parents. Each surface that is touched, held, or gazed at is invested with conscious and unconscious meaning. "The child's body ego is an imaginary anatomy, shaped by the meaning given by the social surrounding and processed by the child" (Harris, 1998, p. 47).

Similarly, each parent's body carries a lifetime of complex meanings, not necessarily verbally symbolizable but unconsciously communicated, transferred into the intersubjective space between them. It is in this parent–child matrix, where the interweaving of intrapsychic and intersubjective experiences come together, that a bodily based subjective experience of gender emerges.

Most recent psychoanalytic theories acknowledge that there are multiple constituents contributing to a child's gendered sense of self. Gender and one's gendered subjectivity are complex processes involving unconscious and conscious fantasies as well as multiple identifications and disidentifications.

De Marneffe's (1997) study of toddlers' understanding of gender and genitals offers a wonderful window through which to begin looking at the construction of gender. She explored how genital experience and knowledge are interpreted by children, what their bodies come to mean to them and how that understanding becomes linked with gender. Her findings suggest that a gendered sense of self may develop quite separately from a genitally based experience of self. This finding is at odds with a fundamental psychoanalytic premise: that the perception of genital difference leads to gender differences. She emphasized that there is no universal, single path or fixed sequence of attaining a sense of gendered subjectivity.

De Marneffe also found that parental naming of genitals, or rather the lack of words to name female genitals for boys and inaccurate naming of female genitals, may suggest parents' anxieties regarding women's bodies. This concurs with Lerner's (1976) dissertation that parents' failure to acknowledge and name the vulva and clitoris contributes to the sense that women don't have permission to be sexually responsive. Family dynamics, values, and attitudes toward gender and genitals clearly play an important role in constructing a child's fantasies and interpretations of their genitals and gender. However, this has seldom been examined. De Marneffe's study is limited by this lack of contextualization and by the use of a homogenous, exclusively heterosexual sample.

Returning, then, to my daughter growing up a White, middle-class lesbian-parented family, we might wonder what it meant to her to say she had a penis. She clearly delighted in the game, in playing with me, in having me on and knowing that she could. In that moment we both knew that she did not have a penis; 10 minutes later she explained that she actually had a vagina and her brother had a penis. Nonetheless, the space to play, to experiment, and to imagine that she could be and do whatever she wanted was welcomed without threatening me or her. Her desire to have the genitals of the other sex seemed more related to their functional capacities and a wish to identify with an older brother. She may have surmised that her older brother's penis gave a sense of greater flexibility and efficiency in the use of the body. It also appears as a playfulness touched with defiance ("I can have and do whatever I want").

Such a way of thinking corresponds with Fast's (1984) insistence on overinclusiveness that explains Horney's (1926) early observation that the concrete interest of a girl in the penis is very different from a regression to penis envy as a result of psychodynamic and often oedipal struggles. In other words, it is important to differentiate the playful fantasy of having a penis from the psychodynamically based wish for a penis. Fogel (1999) has aptly described the latter wish as a fantasy-metaphor or a symbolic fantasy construction. Contemporary theories of gender development place emphasis on relational processes, such as identification and separation rather than genital difference as constitutive of gender identity (Stoller, 1968; Chodorow, 1978; Person and Ovesey, 1983; Fast, 1984; Benjamin, 1991). Benjamin (1991), for example, has articulated the importance of identifications and specifically identificatory love in the development of gender. From this perspective, penis envy is seen as a manifestation of the wish to identify with the father (or the figure outside of the primary parent–infant dyad) as representative of the wish to be recognized as an independent subject, not a concrete wish to have the penis. Tucking his penis behind his thighs, the three-year-old son of my lesbian patient exclaimed, "Look mom, I have a vagina." We came to understand his communication as saying "My body can be like yours, I can be like you, I want to be like you." Similar to my daughter's, his wish for a vagina was the expression of a relational wish rather than a concrete interest in possessing a vagina.

Returning to the importance of the familial context, I would like to expand on the notion of the potential space between parent and child. It is within this rich area of intersubjectivity that many values, attitudes, and taboos are communicated, often quite unconsciously. It also holds the potential for opening up a space for tremendous growth and possibility. Fonagy and Target (1995) have discussed this third perspective as a space belonging to both people and yet to neither person alone. In the relational negotiation between parent and child, gender anxieties are transmitted between each participant. I found myself, in relation to my daughter, tempted to simply say "No, you are not a boy, you're a girl, and it's great to be a girl." With that response, however, I would have been excluding her experience (or fantasy) of being a boy. Bromberg (1998) notes that the degree to which these other voices cannot fully participate in life, they remain alive internally, tormenting the individual and compromising his or her credibility. If health is "the ability to stand in the spaces between realities without losing any of them" (Bromberg, 1998, p. 186), then it takes particularly open, flexible parents to hold onto the multiple realities of gender, to live in them and in the spaces between them.

Gender: To Be a Boy/Girl/Neither
When my daughter told me that she was a boy and a girl, she seemed to be expressing an overinclusive fantasy that all gender possibilities were open to her despite the fact that she couldn't articulate what it meant to be a boy or a girl. It was clear that she perceived the world to be divided into boys and girls, and she did not want to be restricted to the category girl, whatever it might mean. The wish to be a boy or a girl (or both) is expressed by both sexes and has far less to do with gender than with the wish to be unbounded and unlimited (Fast, 1984). Bassin (1996) and Benjamin (1995) diverge from Fast (1984, 1990) in the necessity of renouncing opposite-sex gender identifications and relinquishing the narcissism of bisexuality. Aron (1995), too, advocates that the overinclusive narcissism of the early undifferentiation phase need not be abandoned or renounced but rather integrated with more differentiated positions. As a dialectical interplay, Aron suggests an integration of gender identity with an acceptance of the multiplicity of gender.

We have erred in our psychoanalytic understanding of gender by conflating self identity with gender identity. It therefore seems problematic to me that one would necessarily need to renounce any "gender inappropriate" identifications to establish a core sense of self. It raises the question of what exactly constitutes the "appropriate" gender identity, because there is nothing inherently masculine or feminine. Gender is not a biological given nor inseparable from the maturational process. Femininity and masculinity are social constructs, and therefore what is considered appropriate is constituted by social and historical factors. Consequently, by advocating a gender identity, we are approving a pathological process whereby gender is split into the arbitrary constructs of masculinity and femininity. I do not believe that one has to repudiate psychological attributes to feel human whether we are male or female. As a woman or man we should be free to own any thought, act, feeling, or wish. Having different anatomies should not have to be equated with having to limit, restrict, or abandon any psychological attributes. To accept without contention the splitting of gender into dichotomous terms, and with it the renunciation of that which supposedly belongs to the other sex, is to accept a paranoid-schizoid solution to a self-experience. There is no theoretical need to have a gender identity or to experience ourselves as gendered. I realize that this sounds like a radical concept. It is, and yet it is not. It has been articulated, in one form or another, by several recent deconstructivist theorists, such as Goldner (1991) and Layton (2000).

Goldner exposed that gender, in requiring the "cleansing" of opposing tendencies, is a "universal, false-self system generated in compliance with the rule of the two-gender system" (p. 259). She claims that gender is pathogenic (because of the way that it is constituted through the process of splitting), and therefore she argues against its basic foundational psychoanalytic premise. Layton challenges the notion of cross-gender identifications. According to her, these identifications are capacities that have "nothing to do with gender and are gendered only retrospectively" (p. 57). She notes that it is gender inequality not gender differences that come to define what is deemed masculine or feminine. For her, the cultural problem is not the wish to have it all, but rather the traumatic prescriptions that are enacted by culture on humans limiting what they can feel or think or do. As a clinician, I am aware that we live in a society in which psychological attributes are indeed split along these two apparently opposing gender lines. In our psychoanalytic theorizing, however, we have not been able to move beyond the concept of gender identity and its hierarchically organized gender categories. Nor have we been able to contest gender development.

What I am proposing in this chapter is both idealistic and political. I am pushing the envelope in an attempt to shift the way we understand gender, its organization, purposes, and construction. My idealism stands in creative tension with the cultural necessity of gendering and is linked to a wish for a transformative shift in our conceptualization of gender. I believe that it is through challenging the hegemony of gender that we can find ways to develop more transgressive subjectivities.

Gender Development in Lesbian Families
Studying gender in Australian schools in 1997, Connell and his colleagues have argued that each school can be considered a "gender regime," a conglomeration of structuring processes, whereby different kinds of masculinities and femininities are constructed, ordered, and arbitrated. Similarly one can consider families as gender regimes playing a decisive role in structuring and constructing the organization and meanings of gender. There is surprising variability in the organization and symbolization of gender. To understand this fluctuating significance of gender in social life, we can investigate situations in which gender's salience is more muted or even rendered insignificant. I have chosen lesbian families as a living laboratory of an alternative social structure in which relationships and dynamics of power and difference are not necessarily constructed along gender lines, or solely along gender lines. Lesbian-parented families offer us one alternative paradigm (certainly not the only) from which gender polarities can be transgressed, allowing for the construction of a different form of subjectivity in children. Furthermore, the relationship to gender I am describing is not exclusive to lesbians (nor present in many lesbian relationships), but can be present in any relationship.

There are several ways in which lesbian relationships have the potential to move beyond a simplistic, dichotomized version of gendered parenting. First, if both mothers can accept the multiplicity of their own gender identifications, then it may free their children to see gender as not such a rigid, fixed, and limited construct. Women can be active and passive, they can be strong and weak, they can take care of the finances and fix the light bulb. Gender does not have to determine who does what. In particular, the type of transgressive lesbian family I have in mind is one in which each mother is flexible in her gendered behavior. This may involve feeling comfortable enough to play with gender and to have the internal space to transgress and perform less comfortable stereotypical gender roles.

A precocious five-year-old girl wanted her nonbiological mother to be the "dad." She was drawn to dress-up and role-playing. With friends she would be the damsel in distress, falling in love with the knight in shining armor or she would be the princess marrying her best female friend. Now she wanted a father, and she was insistent. This particular mother, who is creative and introspective, took her request seriously and thought about how to be a "dad." She would dress-up, change her voice to a deeper tone, and even think of more father-like expressions that her daughter might want to hear. She included her child in helping her explore what kind of dad she might want, how that dad would behave, and together they enacted a mother–daughter/father–daughter relationship. To play successfully in this transitional space, the mother needed to be engaged with her own unconscious identifications with masculinity. She also helped her daughter to see that gender is a performance with which one could play. As the nonbiological mother she did not feel threatened by playing the role of father. She did not feel that her daughter needed a male parent and that she, as a woman, was inadequate. She understood that she could be both mother and father, both masculine and feminine. Once again the distinction between anatomy and identifications becomes evident. Whatever was being played out in the family dynamics, her daughter needed her to be something different for a while, with them both understanding that it was role-playing. Yet that transitional space to play, to embrace different identities, to meet each other, was a transformational moment that cemented their bond and helped the child to resolve the issue.

This leads us into the second way in which lesbian relationships may allow for a different organization or symbolization of gender: in the "potential space" between mother and child. In the intersubjective space that belongs to both mother(s) and child and yet neither alone, conscious and unconscious self-states are communicated. As discussed previously, in this mother–child matrix, there is the active involvement with the states of mind of each "other" in the dyad, a cycle of projection, introjection, and projective identification of inner worlds between the participants. If there are self-narratives or states of being that are incompatible with the parent's own gendered self-states, then the child may experience those self-states as "not-me," as discontinuous and thereby split off those unacceptable parts of self. If, however, the mother(s) have more fluid gender identifications and more acceptance of multiple self-states (even if different from those most familiar to self), then the potential space between the two is one of playfulness and growth, a space in which meaning is emergent as a coconstruction between the two participants.

Third, lesbian families may interact in more relaxed, less gender-marked ways. In other words, the meanings of social relations may not be interpreted as gendered. Consequently, this may allow children to express themselves without necessarily identifying the behavior as a gendered experience. Children can identify with their parent as a function of internalizing the multiple aspects of their parents' subjectivity and not simply their gender. Furthermore, we should not forget that the process of identity formation is complex. Maternal identifications are not always feminized in the representation of the self, and similarly paternal identifications are not necessarily masculine identifications. Thus any maternal identification may not be experienced as a feminine identification and may indeed clash with stereotypical maternal gender behaviors. I am not suggesting that it is yet possible to have gender-free identifications. Unfortunately, I think we are so steeped in

a cultural context in which gender is ever present that all identifications may be infused with a gendered flavor, although the
intensity, depth, and saturation levels may have some variability. I do believe, however, that we can move beyond placing
gender in the foreground of all interactions and identificatory
processes.

After a particularly close and bonding morning with his
nonbiological mother, a four-year-old boy exclaimed, "When I
grow up, I want to be a woman just like you." My close friend,
not sophisticated in psychoanalytic theory, intuitively understood his request and replied "When I grow up, I want to be a
boy just like you." It was a moving experience to be watching.
She understood that what he wanted was not an identification
with her as a woman, but with her as a person. He wanted to
be like her, and she returned the compliment to say that she
wanted to be like him. Gender was immaterial. He wanted to
have the attributes of his mother, who happened to be a
woman. She did not respond by saying, when you grow up
you'll be a man, just like your father. She could accept his wish
to be like her independent of gender, although gender was the
medium through which the desire was being expressed.

There has been a long tradition in psychoanalytic theory to
posit the need for the preoedipal father to liberate the child
from the symbiotic attachment with mother. This perpetuates a
splitting along gender lines in which the mother is viewed as
symbolic of attachment and the father represents autonomy
and subjectivity. There is no reason autonomy and subjectivity
should be divided along gender lines. Mothers can be seen as
subjects of desire. This is particularly relevant in lesbian households. It is the function the parent plays rather than his or her
gender that allows for an identification with subjectivity.
Benjamin (1995) has argued that there is no need for the intervention of a "third term" or father symbol to break the maternal dyad and help the child enter the reality of the world.
Rather, recognition and subjectivity can be attained within the
dyad. The third term need not be represented by someone but
"as an effect generated by the symbolic space within a social,
differentiated maternal dyad" (p. 96). According to Benjamin,
father can be viewed as another other, a "second second" but

not as synonymous with the third, which assumes both hetero-sexuality and a single normative form of family. Once again there is a collapsing of subjectivity with gender. The resolution of the original maternal (or paternal)–infant dyad is an issue of subject– subject relations. Instead we resort to the use of gen-der as a force of differentiation and symbol of subjectivity.

Finally, in the construction of subjectivity, it is not simply individual parents who are internalized, but a representation of aspects of their interaction and relationship. These are com-plex relational processes that need not be gendered. These interactional representations include how parents negotiate differences, intimacy, power, and anger (Laing, 1972; Goldner, 1991; Aron, 1995). In a nonhierachical, same-sex relationship in which there is no societally legitimated oppression of one par-ent, the internalization of these interactions can be gender-free. Let us not forget that gender relations are often power rela-tions (Goldner, 1991). Therefore, issues of power between the couple may be more directly experienced rather than express-ing power dynamics through the use of gender. We can gain a far more complex understanding of the dynamics of power without the intervening variable of gender.

Conclusion

It is clear that the construction and dynamics of dichotomized, hierarchically organized gender identities can be restrictive and oppressive, both intrapsychically and culturally. Therefore, in proposing that we give up (at least in theory) the false truth of gender, I am suggesting that we contest the purposes that hav-ing a gender identity serves. Butler (1990) offers the most thor-ough deconstruction of the functions of gender and its production in the cultural discourse:

Gender is, thus, a construction that regularly conceals its gen-esis; the tacit collective agreement to perform produce and sustain discrete and polar genders as cultural fictions is obscured by the credibility of those productions – and the punishments that attend not agreeing to believe in them; the construction compels our belief in its necessity and natural-ness [p. 139].

Butler explains how gender serves the purposes of mandating an idealized, compulsory heterosexuality and male dominance. It is also evident that gender becomes a way in which power, privilege, and various functions are organized between people. It can serve the function of regulating relationships and communications within the family and society. Clearly the meanings of gender are multiple and sometimes contradictory. The salience of gender can be diminished in certain situations, however, one of which is the lesbian-parented family. The presence, significance, and meanings of differences are refocused away from gender when gender is not the primary source of difference between the parents.

Layton (2000) has argued that only by having a type of relating based on mutuality and an awareness of cultural splitting can we produce a transgressive subjectivity. It is worth pondering how development might be different if gender were not the primary lens through which the world were experienced and through which all activities were interpreted. I have tried to explore holding a dialectical tension between an idealistic wish to overthrow the regime of gender with the cultural necessity of gendering.

An important subject for further study would be to situate gender in relation to other lines of difference and inequality. How do the organizations and meanings of gender take shape in relation to other socially constructed divisions such as race and social class? Second, a controlled study with a large sample size would be helpful and valuable. Finally, it should always be remembered that we can never remove ourselves from our sociocultural context. Therefore, even the most open-minded, gender flexible lesbian parents are restricted as the dominant culture imposes its values and mandates gender splitting through unconscious and conscious mechanisms. Nonetheless, I still believe it is worthwhile to find ways to challenge the hegemony of the dominant culture, and as psychoanalysts to never leave a stone unturned. As Domenici and Lesser (1995) remark, psychoanalysis has an opportunity to revitalize itself by contextualizing theory and taking cultural and historical factors into account. It is to the transgressive aspect of psychoanalysis that I aspire.

References

Aron, L. (1995), The internalized primal scene. *Psychoanal. Dial.*, 5:195–237.

Bassin, D. (1946), Beyond the he and she: Postoedipal transcendence of gender polarities. *J. Amer. Psychoanal. Assn.*, 44 (Suppl.):157–189

Benjamin, J. (1991), Father and daughter, identification with difference: A contribution to gender heterodoxy. *Psychoanal. Dial.*, 1:277–299.

———— (1995), *Like Subject, Love Object.* New Haven, CT: Yale University Press.

Bromberg, P. M. (1998), *Standing in the Spaces: Essays on Clinical Process, Trauma and Dissociation.* Hillsdale, NJ: The Analytic Press.

Butler, J. (1990). *Gender Trouble.* New York: Routledge.

Chodorow, N. J. (1978), *The Reproduction of Mothering.* Berkeley: University of California Press.

Coates, S. W. (1997), Is it time to jettison the concept of developmental lines? Commentary on de Marneffe's paper "Bodies and Words." *Gender & Psychoanal.*, 2:35–53.

de Marneffe, D. (1997), Bodies and words: A study of young children's genital and gender knowledge. *Gender & Psychoanal.*, 2:3–33.

Dimen, M. (1998), Polyglot bodies: Thinking through the relational. In: *Relational Perspectives on the Body*, ed. L. Aron & F. S. Anderson. Hillsdale, NJ: The Analytic Press.

Domenici, T. & Lesser, R. C. (1995), *Disorienting Sexuality.* New York: Routledge.

Fast, I. (1984), *Gender Identity.* Hillsdale, NJ: The Analytic Press.

———— (1990), Aspects of early gender development: Toward a reformulation. *Psychoanal. Psychol.*, 7:105–117.

Fogel, G. I. (1999), A postmodern turn for classical metapsychology. In: *Female Sexuality: Contemporary Engagements*, ed. D. Bassin. Northvale, NJ: Aronson, pp. 339–346.

Fonagy, P. & Target, M. (1995), Dissociation and trauma. *Curr. Opin. Psychiat.*, 8:161–166.

Goldner, V. (1991), Toward a critical relational theory of gender. *Psychoanal. Dial.*, 1:481–523.

Harris, A. (1996), Animated conversation: Embodying and engendering. *Gender & Psychoanal.*, 1:361–384.

———— (1998), Psychic envelopes and sonorous baths: Siting the body in relational theory and clinical practice. In: *Relational Perspectives on the Body*, ed. L. Aron & F. S. Anderson. Hillsdale, NJ: The Analytic Press, pp. 39–64.

Horney, K. (1926), The flight from womanhood: The masculinity complex in women, as viewed by men and by women. In: *Feminine Psychology*. New York: W. W. Norton, 1967, pp. 54–70.

Laing, R. D. (1972), *The Politics of the Family*. New York: Vintage Books.

Layton, L. (2000), The psychopolitics of bisexuality. *Studies Gender & Sexual.*, 1:41–60.

Lerner, H. E. (1976), Parental mislabeling of female genitals as a determinant of penis envy and learning inhibitions in women. *J. Amer. Psychoanal Assn.*, 24 (Suppl):269–283.

Person, E. & Ovesey, L. (1983), Psychoanalytic theories of gender identity. *J. Amer. Acad. Psychoanal.*, 11:203–226.

Stoller, R. J. (1968), *Sex and Gender*. New York: Aronson.

Thorne, B. (1997), Children and gender: Constructions of difference. In: *Toward a New Psychology of Gender*, ed. M. M. Gergen & S. N. Davis. New York: Routledge.

3

Couples, Imagined

J. P. Cheuvront

This chapter discusses the clinical treatment of same-gender couples. The purpose, in the simplest sense, is to contribute material about same-gender couples in treatment, but it also addresses the notion of a couple. One cannot begin to think about treating couples without bringing into focus an understanding of what a couple is. This is true regardless of how the couple is gendered. Couples come for treatment with their individual and shared understandings (although not necessarily articulated) of coupled relationships, and these understandings contextualize their immediate concerns. As clinicians, we have our own ideas and experiences of what being a couple means. Clinical facilitation of difficulties occur only when some understanding of the couple's individual and conjoint hopes, fears, and resignations has been made and may require the therapist to question his or her own assumptions of what a couple should look like.

Previous authors have typically focused on specific issues that they feel characterize or are likely to influence same-gender couples, such as coping with HIV (Forstein, 1994; Cabaj and Klinger, 1996), difficulties with autonomy and intimacy (Gray and Isensee, 1996), homophobia (Fisher, 1993; Brown, 1995; Freedman, 1996), and partner abuse (Walsh, 1996). Others have questioned presumptions about differences between same- and discrepant-gender couples (Singer, 1994; MacDonald, 1998) and focused on difficulties imposed by dominant societal ideas of intimate relationships with emphases on a broader understanding of what constitutes a couple (Simon, 1996). In my own experience, same- and discrepant-gender couples do not look particularly different in treatment. Specific concerns, whether they are struggles with an illness (such as HIV or cancer) or social intrusions (such as racism, sexism, or homophobia), must (and can only) be understood from within the perspective of the couple under treatment.

Although an increasingly significant portion of psychoanalytically informed clinical treatment is being conducted with couples, with few notable exceptions (i.e., Trop, 1994; Gerson, 1996; Sander, 1998) surprisingly little of the clinical and theoretical literature is devoted to case examples, clinical technique, and theoretical understandings of couples work. Much of the writings on couples treatment is found in or influenced by the family therapy literature. My own theoretical disposition focuses on the intersubjective (e.g., Stolorow, Brandchaft, and Atwood, 1987; Stolorow and Atwood, 1992; Orange, Atwood, and Stolorow, 1997) nature of interpersonal relations. Intersubjective refers to the relational contexts in which experience emerges (Stolorow, Orange, and Atwood, 1999) — in which personal experience is seen as fluid, multidimensional, context-sensitive, and historically influenced — to my mind a distinct and much broader meta-theoretical conceptualization than that of mutual recognition, as it is used elsewhere in the literature (e.g., Stern, 1985; Benjamin, 1995).

Intersubjective approaches to couples therapy have been outlined previously. Trop (1994, 1997) has discussed the importance of understanding disjunctive interactions within couples by illuminating the principles unconsciously organizing the participants' inner experiences. Ringstrom (1994) suggests that partner's tendency to reenact conflictual past events in the service of maintaining self organization is important in couple's understanding each other and their relational difficulties. The idea that conflicts arise from the negotiation of hoped-for and feared responses rooted in early experiences and that articulation of these dynamics is important in couples treatment has been recognized and elaborated on by Alexander and Van Der Heide (1997) and McMahon (1997).

Each of these authors has used intersubjectivity to explain conflicts that arise within relationships and how the understandings of these conflicts can be used clinically to more closely approximate a truth for the couple that effects change in the quality of their interactions and understanding of their partnership. Implicit in each of these articles, and indeed in much of the couples therapy literature, is the notion that the couple, as the entity under treatment and as a treatment goal, is a shared, understood concept between the individuals in treatment and between therapist and patients. Often unsaid are presumptions about coupled relationships as particularly gendered, structurally and temporally stable, and context-insensitive. Left unquestioned and unarticulated, these discrepancies can cause distance, misunderstandings, and disruptions within the couple, as well as between the couple and therapist. What has not been discussed, to my knowledge, is how intersubjectivity, a meta-theory that specifically looks at the subjective experiences that influence psychological theorists' understandings and development of their own theories, can help us understand how our own beliefs about couples might facilitate, hinder, or otherwise influence and guide treatment of couples.

Using case material, this chapter illustrates how clinical dialogue can facilitate articulation of the patient's lived experiences, and how expansion of each of the partner's capacity to understand and empathize with both their own and their spouse's experiences can usher in change. Of particular importance in the clinical exchange are the individuals' understandings of what it means to be a couple. This includes hoped-for and feared experiences, disappointments, negotiation and experiences of social support (or disapproval), and the perceived (wished-for or dreaded) degree to which the notion of being coupled limits or expands the domain of shared and personal experiences. The chapter also demonstrates how viewing the notion of a couple as constructed by the participants provides a context from which a wide breadth of solutions and ways of understanding difficulties can be articulated. If one is going to "treat" a construct, if a construct is seeking assistance, then it is vitally important that the construction, the troubled interpersonal field, this virtual patient, be understood. And it is here, in our willingness and capacity to meet our patient's struggles and creative approaches to sharing their lives with others that notions of gender configuration quickly recede and more salient dynamics of lived experiences emerge.

Christopher and Stuart
There was a lot of catching-up to do: Christopher and Stuart, 49 and 50 years old, respectively, had been together for 18 years when they first came to seek treatment. By profession, they were writer and publisher. Stuart met Christopher when the small publishing company where he was working published one of Christopher's books in the early 1980s. This marked the beginning of a personal and professional relationship which had, despite setbacks, endured to the present time. Treatment commenced on the heels of a whirlwind 18 months in which they had busied themselves producing one of Christopher's short novels for television, the first joint venture for the company they had established together. Besides a rigorous production schedule and frequent trips to shoot locations, Christopher and Stuart had managed to see Stuart through a major medical crisis related to his diet-controlled diabetes that required a week's stay in the hospital and substantial rehabilitation on discharge. All of this was achieved without modification or setback in the production schedule. In fact, they recounted, their sponsoring agency and crew only became aware of the personal crisis after the production was completed.

Crisis, in the form of extreme productivity, was not what brought this couple to treatment. As a team, Christopher and Stuart were particularly skilled at tackling adversity. Earlier in their relationship, a time characterized by frequent parties, lavish spending, and frequent drug and alcohol use, Christopher and Stuart had helped each other confront their substance abuse problems. They established a sobriety that both had sustained for more than 10 years. Much more difficult for both of them was down time — periods that were outside of crisis and when the pressures of productivity were reduced, which by design, should have been times when they could enjoy the fruit of their labors. Instead, they reported fighting and bickering of a sort they never experienced while busy and complained that they had difficulty finding leisure activities they both enjoyed. This surprised and worried them both because they had spent count-less hours anticipating the end of the most recent project as a time to relax with each other, spend time with friends, and attend to their neglected personal lives.

The first two months of treatment were spent warming to one another. They depicted themselves as the "model couple" in their circle of friends, an impression that did not surprise me given their seeming ease with one another, clever banter, and complementary charm. In our initial sessions, little of the con-flict they were describing in the content of their narratives was apparent in their interpersonal interactions. Christopher and Stuart would describe bickering escalating to verbal fighting and profoundly hurt feelings, although their behavior betrayed little to none of this within the treatment process.

After this period, they began a series of disagreements in treatment. The session began as usual, with a recounting of the previous week's events. To meet financial obligations, Stuart had taken a consulting position for a publisher that afforded them a steady income in the interim between their own projects. They had agreed that Christopher would attend to their busi-ness, which at this point consisted of the relatively mundane tasks of producing financial reports and sorting out expenses for the recently completed project. As of late, Stuart had been busier than usual, preoccupied with a publishing deadline that was fast approaching. Shared time had been reduced to the few hours before sleep, which often took the form of an exhausted Stuart planting himself in front of the television. The television had long been a source of disagreement, with Stuart finding the passive entertainment relaxing and Christopher experiencing the drone of the tube as intrusive and extremely irritating in a small apartment that afforded no means of escape.

As Stuart and Christopher recounted their disagreement, Christopher became increasingly withdrawn, more careful than usual about his word choices, and seemingly preoccupied with an internal struggle that communicated a sense of hopelessness and isolation. Stuart responded by appearing exasperated and angry at Christopher's distance. Whereas I had previously seen Stuart reach out to Christopher when struggling with depressive affect, here he made no such effort. As the discussion continued, interpersonal distance widened, and the content turned toward Christopher's concerns about Stuart's health and his worry that he was not taking proper care of himself. Stuart responded with irritation, noting feelings of intrusiveness and vulnerability. He described feeling that in these moments Christopher was "hitting below the belt." Christopher understood this as confirmation that his concerns about Stuart's health, including his fear that he alone was worried about Stuart's physical condition, were justified. He also took this as indication that their partnership was severely troubled.

This, they would confirm later, was the typical resting place of their "downward spiral." Arguments would invariably shift to usher in and heighten feelings of distance, hopelessness, intrusiveness, and a sense of unresolve. Our session ended on this note, a silence lingering between the three of us as, I imagined, they reflected on their frustration and difficult feelings evoked by this too-often repeated discourse pattern. I reflected on the hopefulness of having been allowed to witness the interpersonal knots they had previously only described.

The following session showed none of the difficulty or interpersonal distance of the prior session. Both Stuart and Christopher were able to reflect on their experience of the session, including the experience of my presence. They agreed that they had both been conscious of my presence during their exchange and had alternately wondered when I was going to "step up and fix things" and whether their difficulties were too overwhelming for me. I told them that I could understand how they could have these experiences given the clear distress that they both had experienced. I then summarized as best I could what I experienced as their individual emotional states and concerns during their interchange.

Over the course of the next four months, weekly treatment continued to move forward. Sessions regularly repeated the same degenerative, dead-end form displayed previously, and other sessions consisted of reflecting and articulating their dynamics as a couple and as individuals. During these times, my interest often focused on dimensions of their individual life experiences, particularly experiences in relationships outside their partnership. I also took opportunities to become more familiar with their understandings of intimate relationships in their families of origin.

My inquiries into Christopher's and Stuart's individual familial experiences stemmed from material they provided. For example, the death of Stuart's brother and their visit with the family ushered in a host of memories and reflections about his family life as a child. In our dialogue, I learned of the intrusive nature of Stuart's father, the struggle of his mother to feel some semblance of control, and the potential explosive (literally) nature of family discussions. Broken windows, physical altercations, and banishments from the home were not uncommon. Relationships, as displayed by Stuart's parents, were coercive, undermining, and volatile. Concern for others was always viewed with skepticism and suspicion, subject to scrutiny for ulterior motives. Concurrently, a love between parents, siblings, and other family members was often displayed. They were fiercely protective of their own and had, in very specific ways, demonstrated profound devotion to one another. The net result was that feelings of love comingled with the potential for harm. Members of the family were protected from outside dangers, but internal destruction was often tolerated or overlooked.

Inquiry into Christopher's feelings of hopelessness and fear of isolation from Stuart recalled a period in his late teens when he was hospitalized for nine months for a treatable, but severe, medical condition that required the attention of experts in a town miles from his childhood home. During this time difficulties arose elsewhere in his family that compounded the physical distance with emotional unavailability. Initially, relatives who lived close to the hospital provided support. This support faded, however, as in Christopher's recollection, he increasingly expressed his distress at the little attention and emotional support he was receiving from his family. As such, Christopher dreads feelings of abandonment and his own expression of needs. Experience has told him that this is met with further isolation and increasing despair.

As Stuart's and Christopher's individual histories became elaborated, I began to weave these understandings into the treatment. I became better able to articulate the felt difficulties encountered at the depths of their arguments as old feelings and fears rooted in early family interactions. Christopher's feelings of profound hopelessness and emotional abandonment were tied to his early feelings from the actual withdrawal of familial support during the crisis of his late adolescence. His desperation in the face of these feelings understandably caused him to become excited and express his concerns, needs, and fears to Stuart. In turn, Stuart experienced Christopher as argumentative and found the intensity of his experiences frightening. It was, for Stuart, the sort of intense emotional milieu that led to physical violence and emotional destructiveness within his family. Stuart's response was to withdraw protectively, dodging the literal blows he imagined would inevitably follow. Of course these sorts of dynamics are cyclic — Stuart's withdrawal in the face of Christopher's expressed emotional experience only induced increased panic in Christopher and furthered Stuart's withdrawal. This was the heart of the downward spiral.

Over the course of three or four sessions, Christopher, Stuart, and I worked to understand and articulate these dynamics. Although the initial introduction of my understandings occurred during sessions in which the dynamics were in action, subsequent sessions inevitably led to reviewing the session with more emotional distance. During these sessions, both patients made modifications and refinements, and both attempted to articulate their partner's position, or as we came to describe it, their dilemma. Eventually, my interpretations became their dialogue. It was clear that the elaboration of these ideas had taken on a life of its own outside of treatment — to the point that it became common for me to ask them to help me catch up. Concurrently, the frequency and intensity of their arguments tended to diminish. Arguments became disagreements and, at times, opportunities to understand one another better.

Within treatment, the degenerative, dead-end, affect-laden arguments were replaced by discussions of fears, dilemmas, dissatisfactions, and pleasures of their intimate and business partnership. Whereas difficulties in conducting their business had been a major motivating factor in bringing Christopher and Stuart into treatment, early attempts at discussing these issues had quickly led to misunderstandings, misattunements, and, ultimately (once they felt comfortable enough to do this in front of me), degenerative argumentation. At this point in treatment, they were able to articulate their concerns more productively. Nonetheless, the presenting dilemma — that they were unable to settle on down-time activities that they enjoyed doing together — continued to bother them. For a period of time, we discussed possible solutions to this problem, including activities that they might both find enjoyable. For example, we discussed how a short trip to a location that both Christopher and Stuart enjoyed might provide some mutual enjoyment and feeling of togetherness. In my treatment experience, it is unusual for these sorts of suggestions to, unto themselves, address the underlying feelings of dissatisfaction. Couples are rarely so naïve or uncreative as to be unable to problem solve, on their own, pragmatic difficulties. In the context of treatment, however, couples often expect this sort of problem solving with the therapist and perceive it as an engagement in process that they can easily recognize as "working on the relationship." From my perspective, problem solving is useful because it can help facilitate and strengthen working relational ties between the therapist and patients. When this works, I believe it is because we have optimally responded (Bacal, 1998) to the couple's needs, not that we have provided such a brilliant pragmatic solution.

As we struggled in treatment with the frustration Stuart and Christopher felt at having what looked like discrepant (and, at times, opposing) ways of spending free time, it occurred to me that what had been left unquestioned were the sources and reasons for their frustration. Why, I wondered, was it so important for Stuart and Christopher to spend their free time with each other, particularly when a large percentage of their time was spent together negotiating their business? The idea that free time should or must be spent with one's spouse and that somehow the camaraderie, mutuality, and team effort that occurs in the context of "work" is different than or inferior to shared experiences in free time is often a misconception. This presumption about the use of free time is related, I think, to an idea that our culture seems to hold in which it is presumed that all of an individual's interpersonal needs to be provided by his or her spouse (S. Kiersky, 1999, personal communication). It is, I believe, often stronger than the tradition of sexual fidelity in that feelings of betrayal are clearly worsened when a cheating spouse is revealed to have, in addition to being sexually unfaithful, spent free time (for example, vacations) with the lover, with the implication being that these moments were robbed from the rightful recipient. More realistically, individual needs are varied and change over time. What is certain about the reification of the spouse as the sole provider of companionship, friendship, and other interpersonal needs is that eventually needs will go unmet. This is not to say that for some couples the inability to engage in mutually enjoyable activities is not problematic. But for Christopher and Stuart, whom I had often heard speak about their work together with excitement, I genuinely felt that the quality of their work time together was experienced as quite profound, sustaining, and rewarding for them both.

The opportunity to introduce the kernel of this idea was presented in a session in which they again expressed their concern about competing wishes as to ways to spend nonwork time:

JPC: You know, despite our efforts to come up with some ways you might enjoy each other's company during less busy times, there continues to be some dissatisfaction with the quality of the time you spend with each other, and today you both sound a little hopeless about it. [Stuart and Christopher both nod in agreement.] I wonder if it might help for us to think a little differently about the dilemma. I guess I'm trying to understand why, for both of you, you feel that this is an important dilemma to solve.

CHRISTOPHER: [Lightheartedly] Well, it would be nice if we could just have a regular relationship and enjoy each other when we're not overloaded with the insanity of work.

STUART: [Agreeing] It would just be nice if we didn't have the arguments and bickering during off time.

JPC: [Roused by Stuart's idea of "regular relationship"] Yeah, and we've seen how it really affects the quality of your time together. But I guess I'm interested in something Christopher said. I'm not sure you realized it, but you said you wanted to have a "regular relationship." [Smiles all around as everyone seems to understand, in the context of a same-gender relationship, this is a humorous notion.] What do you think you mean by this?

CHRISTOPHER: Well, I guess I don't really mean "regular."

JPC: But I think you were getting at something quite specific that is not so easy to articulate. I know you don't mean that you want a woman partner, but it seems like there might be some other idea there.

CHRISTOPHER: Well, I guess I look at other couples and they like to do things together. They have mutual interests, like they like to go to the movies together, or do sports together, or go dancing, or something. We seem to have such trouble in that sense. It makes me feel that we must be such a poor match, and that when we are working we are just too busy to notice.

JPC: So, your different ways of wanting to enjoy free time sort of stokes a fear that you are not, in fact, a good match?

CHRISTOPHER: Yeah, and it makes me sort of sad, because I would love to share these things with Stuart.

JPC: So there is a kind of loneliness that is part of this as well. Stuart, what are your thoughts?

STUART: I understand what Chris is talking about, for him, I think this really bothers him. I guess that I'm just mostly bothered by his dissatisfaction. I'm caught sometimes wondering whether I agree but don't want to think about us being a bad match, or whether it's just not true and he's making something of nothing. I mean, [to Christopher] I'm not saying you are making it up, I know you feel this way, and I understand that, it's just that I don't think I feel the same pressure. I guess there is so much that we do share that it doesn't have the same feeling to me.

JPC: How do you mean, Stuart?

STUART: Well, look what we've been through. We got sober together, we published together, we went broke together, we made a television show, we have lectured together, we got through my hospitalization. I just think that whether we agree on a movie to see or whether to go to a museum together isn't that important.

JPC: So for you the work you do together sort of sustains the feelings of closeness, but Christopher seems to have other expectations.

CHRISTOPHER: Well, I agree with Stuart. I don't know, it just seems like we should enjoy doing things together that aren't work related. [Pause] Also, if I don't do them with Stuart, I don't do these things at all. Like I never saw [my friend's] exhibit at the [museum].

JPC: So it feels like, if you don't do something with Stuart you can't do it at all, like with someone else?

CHRISTOPHER: I guess I could. I mean, that's the way it seems to play out.

JPC: Maybe what we should be talking about and trying to understand, then, is not so much about finding ways that the two of you can be comfortable and enjoy free time together, but how you can be comfortable and enjoy free time apart.

Subsequently, Christopher and Stuart have been able to articulate a broader range of experiences within these interactions. For example, Christopher has linked his fear that Stuart might become emotionally distant as a factor that motivates the desire for shared down time. He has noticed that this is connected to feelings of being controlled by Stuart in that his unavailability for a particular experience has the impact of essentially preventing Christopher from engaging in the event. Rather than simply experience this as Stuart's wielding of control, Christopher has begun to understand how his own fears contribute to a context in which his options become limited. Similarly, Stuart has been better able to understand Christopher's frustration and how, at times, his unwillingness to alleviate Christopher's fears about their relationship plays an important part in Christopher's unwillingness to seek out friends with shared interests.

In general, our discourse has changed focus. We have moved from feelings of general dissatisfaction and unease to a dialogue in which specific affective experiences and ideas about historical sources can be connected. This historical awareness helps to explain and make understandable the emotional intensity of interpersonal difficulties. This is, I think, at the heart of what is meant by a deepening of the treatment — an idea often invoked when discussing individual treatment but less commonly used to describe the process of couples treatment. The intersubjectivity literature describes these clinically facilitating conditions as a broadening of experience in individual treatment: "closer and closer approximations of such truths are gradually achieved through an analytic dialogue in which the domain of reflective self-awareness is enlarged for both participants" (Stolorow, Atwood, and Orange, 1999, p. 387). Replace the words *both participants* with the words *all participants* and you have, from my perspective, a fairly accurate description of an important process active in all meaningful couples work. A process that expands the domain of possibility, limited only by the participants' abilities to stretch beyond social convention and preciously held fantasies about the structure of hoped-for relationships. As Stuart and Christopher's case suggests, in couples therapy with same-gender couples, treatment can move quite quickly beyond the couple's gender configuration. Rather, as in struggles within any intimate relationship, articulation of closer and closer approximations of mutual and individual lived experiences helps create a context in which feelings of difficulty, confusion, hopelessness, and anxiety can be reduced — made to feel understandable, tenable, and ultimately assuaged.

Simone and Deborah

Many couples come to treatment when they realize that channels of communication are failing and emotional experiences or situational factors (or both) overwhelm their capacities to cope. This was the case with Simone and Deborah, aged 42 and 37, respectively, who came for treatment five years into their relationship. Some details of their treatment show the ways in which hoped-for or expected life experiences, bolstered by the pressures of social norms, can be a focal point of friction within a couple. This may limit their capacity for intimacy and mutuality. Their case illustrates how couples treatment can illuminate the couple's ever-shifting meanings of these struggles to help articulate, broaden, and demystify their individual and shared lived experiences.

Simone met Deborah two years after her divorce from a marriage that had produced two children, Shawn and Mark. They have lived primarily with Simone, but spend significant time with their father, who shares joint custody and lives in the same neighborhood. At present Shawn and Mark are aged 14 and 12, respectively. One year into their relationship, Deborah moved in with Simone and her family, effectively becoming a stepparent to the boys. This was a welcomed role for Deborah who, having envisioned starting her own family someday, jumped at the opportunity to parent. In couples sessions, Deborah confirmed that this opportunity was an important factor that attracted her to Simone. Unfortunately, in important ways the role of stepparent was more difficult than Deborah had expected. Although she had forged a strong bond with Simone's youngest son Mark early in their relationship, relations with his older brother Shawn proved to be much more difficult. Shawn, aged 10 when Deborah moved in with the family, had proven to be a dispositionally difficult child. Precocious to a fault, Shawn was prone to mood swings and to lashing out verbally at others unexpectedly. His strong capacity to articulate his thoughts and feelings made him capable of being hurtful while at the same time radiating a charm that attracted peers and adults alike. This was not lost on Deborah, who felt unwelcome and rejected by Shawn while hoping for acceptance and the sort of close bond she had forged with his younger brother.

From Deborah's perspective, the first four years of the relationship were spent deepening her relationship with Mark while attempting to forge a relationship with Shawn. Difficulties increased between Deborah and Shawn as the boy entered adolescence. Shawn's behavior began to feel more provocative and mean-spirited, often targeting Deborah or Simone. Whereas Simone tended toward tolerance, understanding, and nonconfrontation, Deborah was dispositionally more structured, suggesting to Deborah that greater limits, rules, and more frequent discussions with Shawn about his misbehavior were crucial. Deborah's distance from Shawn and the difficulties living in the same home with him added fire to her wish for direct action in the form of rules and punishments. Simone, who had the advantage of confidence in her connection to her son, disagreed, suggesting that Deborah needed to be more understanding of Shawn and his moody nature.

Four months prior to the start of treatment, Deborah had had enough. Weary of her ability to forge a relationship with Shawn, aggravated by her feeling of being relegated to second-tier parent, and increasingly experiencing herself as a visitor in her own home, Deborah suggested that she and Simone separate. Simone was not entirely sure this was a bad idea. For her part, she had found Deborah to be increasingly withdrawn, spending much of the time and energies previously devoted to the family on activities and interests away from the home. Simone understood this as evidence of Deborah's selfishness and unwillingness to compromise for the family and had experienced her lack of engagement and distance as worrisome. Attempts at discussing the precariousness of their situation quickly degenerated into hurtful arguments and furthered mutual withdrawal. Despite their disagreements, both Simone and Deborah were fearful of losing the other. In the spirit of working out a way to be together, they agreed that including a mediator in the form of a couples therapist might help them better understand their difficulties and maintain their relationship.

Throughout treatment Deborah's feelings of disappointment with her parental role coupled with Simone's feeling that Deborah was unwilling to give up her own needs for the family emerged as central points of contention. The meaning of parenting and the negotiation of parental roles in the family, however, shifted for the couple through the course of treatment. To trace these themes as they developed through the treatment, I will show how the parenting disagreement emerged in the course of three successive periods in treatment and how it served as a venue within which different kinds of relational difficulties could be illuminated and understood.

Our attempts at discussing the couple's dissatisfactions echoed the stalemate that brought them into treatment. No sooner did Deborah touch on her feelings of frustration in her role as parent, particularly with Shawn, than Simone responded by seemingly tuning out Deborah's concerns and by shifting the conversation to her own feeling that Deborah was selfish and "wants things both ways." The disagreement was clearly stale, both participants having approached the topic from any number of ways over the past years. I was most impressed with how the interaction showed the degree to which Deborah and Simone had difficulty hearing each other's concerns without becoming defensive. Although absent from the actual content of their discussion, the notion of a responsible party and blame seemed to be ever present and implicit in the process of their discourse. As with Christopher and Stuart, moving treatment further relied on helping the couple find a way to discuss matters such that they could actually listen to each other without the distraction of raising defenses. It is difficult to be empathic when one is feeling threatened.

To this end, our conversation moved to better understanding the feelings that emerged when they attempted to discuss parenting disagreements, rather than resolving the matter itself. Inquiry inevitably led to individual histories and emotional experiences, hopes, and fears with caretakers. Treatment illuminated an underlying lack of trust, rooted in early experiences, for both Simone and Deborah. Distrust emerged from a proclivity to stoke one another's fears based on self-protective measures that inadvertently fueled a complementary, and equally provoking, reaction from the other partner. We identified these interactions as rooted in their individual and discrepant experiences with early caregivers and their attempts to head off similar dreaded experiences in their current relationship. As in the prior case material, our discourse seemed to provide a way in which Simone and Deborah could better empathize with each other, allowing them to feel less provoked or attacked by their partner, and sympathize with the other's internal struggles. Only with this established could they to actually begin to hear and entertain each other's concerns about their relationship, family, and individual lives.

This period in treatment, although brief in the telling, unfolded over three to four months of weekly sessions. There is no substitute for time, particularly with integrating new understandings of their partner's lives, couples require continued work out of sessions. Simone and Deborah were active in this respect, often reporting how they had disentangled themselves during disagreements at home. For Simone and Deborah (as with many couples in therapy), the relief felt at this point in treatment had a direct impact on improving the quality of their daily lives. It is at this point that couples report that the "tools" therapy provided have made the sort of arguments that brought them into treatment a thing of the past. Unfortunately, for some couples this relief reduces their motivation for treatment just as their ability to engage one another's emotional experiences becomes available. Particularly for couples in which both individuals are petrified of life without their relationship, the removal of these polarizing arguments can be experienced as threatening.

However frightened they may have felt about losing a future together, Simone and Deborah continued treatment. Deborah reintroduced complaints of dissatisfaction with the parenting role following an incident between her and Shawn, witnessed by Simone, in which she felt hurt by Shawn's verbal lashing out and unsupported by Simone's reluctance to intervene:

DEBORAH: . . . I feel like my hands are tied, and you [Simone] don't do anything to make it easier.

JPC: What sort of things from Simone would help?

DEBORAH: If we could come from a unified front. She should have stepped in and said, "Shawn, it's inappropriate to talk to someone like that."

Simone: But I didn't hear him as attacking you: it felt like he was angry at both of us.

DEBORAH: No, it was definitely pointed at me. When he said [something directly relevant to Deborah's actions that day in their house], he clearly was singling me out. And it's hurtful to hear it from him and frustrating to not be able to do anything about it.

JPC: What would you like to do?

DEBORAH: Well, I would like to say, "Shawn, that's inappropriate to say to someone, you're being rude, nasty, and hurtful." But I can't do it, or at least I'm not supposed to do it according to [Shawn's therapist].

Simone: I thought that we agreed with [Shawn's therapist] that the discipline shouldn't come from you.

DEBORAH: Yeah, we did. But it's hard.

JPC: It can't be easy having someone who lives in your house verbally attacking you without having any recourse.

DEBORAH: Yes. It would help if Simone could step in at those times, so it wouldn't have to be me but it would be handled anyway.

JPC: It might also communicate to you that Simone understood the awkwardness of your position and is trying to help.

SIMONE: I don't have a problem with that. It's just that sometimes, like this, I don't really have a sense that Deborah has been hurt. Until she told me now, I didn't know that she felt more targeted any more than me.

JPC: That is something you need to work on. See, I sense that the reason Simone is less likely to be ruffled by Shawn has to do with the strength of their relationship — when Shawn isn't in one of his "moods," Simone and Shawn can be buddies, she is his confidant. I think that creates a willingness to forgive or ignore some of the difficult parts of Shawn. [They both nod in agreement.] I think it is much more difficult for Deborah, who imagines her parental relationship as more like the one she has with Mark, and given how distant Shawn keeps from her, Shawn and Deborah's relationship is more like roommates who don't really like each other than like parent and child.

SIMONE: Is that how if feels to you?

DEBORAH: Yeah, it's like a bad college roommate, but you don't have to take your college roommate to soccer practice.

This excerpt represents an important turn in Simone and Deborah's relationship. Not only is Simone able to begin to understand Deborah's difficulty with Shawn, but they both begin to see that Simone's seeming unwillingness to intervene may, in fact, not suggest lack of caring for her spouse (as Deborah fears) but a different subjective experience that has limited her capacity to attune herself to Deborah's struggle. Specifically, Simone is able to hear and understand through the roommate metaphor the discomfort Deborah is experiencing in her daily life. The discrepancy in their capacities to tolerate Shawn's difficult moments is understood through the parental affirmation Shawn bestows on Simone but denies to Deborah. Through conversations like these in subsequent sessions, Simone and Deborah clarified other points of contention.

Simone's feeling that Deborah was selfish and unwilling to give up certain aspects of her life for the family began to be understood as ways that Simone had begun to compensate for needs not provided within the family, and how these outside activities actually helped her cope with her mixed feelings about her parental role.

For both Deborah and Simone, these new understandings competed with their individual fantasized versions of their relationship. For Deborah, the hoped for relationship with Simone was one in which she felt fully engaged as an equal parent, beloved by both her spouse and her adopted children. The actual complexities and contingencies of her lived experience ran counter to this, partially by not accounting for the common awkwardness of being a stepparent, and partially by the perceived threat and concomitant provocative protective measures made by Shawn. Feeling increasingly anxious and hopeless about the widening gulf between her hoped for and lived experience, Deborah had sought an explanation. Attempts at discussing this with Simone raised Simone's anxiety, preventing her from helping Deborah understand the situational factors that precluded the hoped-for experience. Unable to see this and faced with Simone's defensiveness, Deborah experienced Simone as unresponsive, uncaring, and ultimately responsible for her unsatisfactory parenting experience. Only when Simone and Deborah felt safe enough to listen to one another were they able to see the broader context influencing their difficulties.

Simone's ideal of an untroubled spousal relationship required similar attention to the broader impact of their circumstances. Simone experienced Deborah's dissatisfactions as childish and as reflecting an unrealistic wish to both be involved in the family and have a life outside of the family as well. Simone experienced Deborah's outside interests as contrary to her professed hopes for their family and, in this respect, often felt that she had to negotiate Deborah as a third demanding child. She did not understand that Deborah needed to use outside activities as a way of counterbalancing her experience of parenting as disappointing and that Deborah's experience as a stepparent was different from her own as a birth parent. As such, Deborah's complaints and absences stood contrary to Simone's imagined relationship for her and her family. As with Deborah, increased capacity for listening to one another shifted this understanding, providing her access to the complexities of her partner and broadening the domain of her own experience.

Both of these themes, Deborah's feelings about parenting and Simone's idea about her spouse's relationship within the family, continued to be discussed in treatment. Once they began to understand and articulate one another's experiences, both Deborah and Simone were faced with the decision as to whether they were willing to give up their hoped-for experiences and engage in the present circumstance, or whether they wished to part ways and pursue other partners with whom they might find the desired conditions. Either decision requires giving up something, either the lived relationship or the hoped-for relational configuration. This sort of dilemma can be overwhelming for couples. Often individuals require access to their own treatment to understand what they are giving up. This was the case for Deborah, who on extensive reflection announced the following near the end of the couples treatment:

DEBORAH: [to Simone] You know that I still want to feel like an equal parent, but I guess I understand the sort of things that stand in the way of it. It's not that I'm not hoping for more, but I think somehow I hadn't really considered everything.

JPC: What do you mean?

DEBORAH: Well, like my relationship with Mark.

JPC: You mean, that you feel like that is a good relationship?

DEBORAH: Yeah. Especially after [an event the previous week in which the importance of Deborah to Mark was quite apparent].

JPC: Are there other things?

DEBORAH: Well, my relationship with Simone. [To Simone] I think that we've sort of overlooked us. The kids are such a big part of things now, but as I think about it, in less than six years Shawn will probably be out of the house, and then in a few more Mark will be gone, and that ultimately it's you and me.

SIMONE: That's hard to imagine, but you're right.

JPC: So, how does that impact on you now?

DEBORAH: Well, I was talking to [my therapist] and I asked myself, am I happy? Not in general, just today, am I happy today? And the answer was yes. Things are great with Mark, Simone and I are arguing less and less and getting better at discussing things. And even with Shawn, with his therapy, I feel like there are some changes that are occurring. And like we've talked about, who knows what sort of relationship we might have in the future. So I guess that means I am here for now, and it feels okay making that day-to-day decision, it helps me appreciate what I do have and takes me away from focusing on some idea of how things should be.

This segment illustrates the beginning of Deborah's capacity to integrate expected feelings with her actual experiences. Similarly, Simone has been able to see how Deborah cannot provide hopes for her spousal relationship. Through treatment, Simone has struggled to integrate her idea of how an intimate relationship should appear with the actual lived experience with Deborah. She has started to understand how Deborah's absence is less a reflection of her feelings for Simone, but an attempt to provide meaningful experiences for herself that are not fulfilled by her parenting role. Faced with this fuller view of their shared experience, Deborah and Simone are left to weigh the benefits and pitfalls of remaining together and separating.

In general, Deborah and Simone entered treatment clutching ideas about their relationship that, given their circumstances, could not possibly be met by one another. Their discourse surrounding difficulties in parenting provided the context through which they were able to negotiate and better understand their struggles. Early attempts at understanding these difficulties pointed to their inability to listen to or empathize with one another's experiences. Treatment at this point focused on helping the couple better communicate through identifying fears and feelings that seemed to get in the way when attempting to discuss emotionally laden topics. Once they became better able to listen to one another, discussions about their parenting difficulties focused on articulating and understanding the contexts that gave rise to their circumstance and questioning their fears and assumptions about their partner's intentions. These discussions pointed out the inevitable clash between their hoped-for relationship and actual lived experience. Later in treatment, discussions about parenting and their relationship changed focus to expressions of mourning about lost aspects of the hoped-for relationship and recognition of pleasures and satisfactions in their lived experiences.

Discussion
We all hold preconceived ideas about intimate relationships, including how they are gendered. Hopes and concerns about interactions with others are formed starting with our earliest experiences. The idea of a couple emerges in our experiences with caregivers and is elaborated by social and cultural influences as we increasingly have contact with the outside world in childhood. These interactions are complex. Wished-for experiences from caregivers originating in childhood can remain a central influence on people's adult assessment of intimate relationships long after the wished-for experiences have lost their importance. Similarly, feared experiences of intimate relationships, rooted in childhood, can narrow the adult's capacity to take risks, feel comfortable with commitment, or be available for closeness and mutuality. These organizing influences, both from caregivers and our culture, can go unnoticed while exerting tremendous impact on the course of our lives. This is often the material of individual therapy. That this is also important material for couples therapy should not be surprising. An additional complexity is introduced in couples therapy, however, in that precisely that which we are supposed to treat — namely, the couple — is elusive. We are assisted in individual treatment, I suspect, by our physical boundaries that render agreement as to the meaning of individual in all but the most unusual, and often severe, cases. Differences in subjective experiences between the members of the couple and the therapist introduce at least three sets of mutually influenced understandings about couples. As I hope the two cases presented here have shown, an important aspect of couples therapy is the articulation, understanding, and, if possible, integration of these experiences.

Resolution in couples therapy can occur when competing unfulfilled hopes and concerns have been identified. The clinical dialogue, when focused on articulating the participants' felt experiences, evokes closer and closer approximations of subjective truths about their lived experiences together. Unfortunately, integration of opposing desires and fears is a process marked by access to new experiences, and thus, a function of time. As a result, predictions about the outcome of an individual's or couple's struggle are difficult to make. My own experience suggests that although couples therapy can diminish the time spent approaching a resolution to these struggles, it has less impact on the desired outcome. This is to say that couples therapy can hope to illuminate the struggles faced by the couple, but cannot take the couple's or therapist's ideals about successful partnering as criteria for success. Couples therapy can only serve to clarify certain aspects of the patients' lived experiences, leaving full integration or disposal of certain aspects for the future.

Couples, however they are imagined, however they are gendered, come to therapy because there is unhappiness, there is anxiety, there is conflict. The vantage point of the couples therapist is only as expansive as our capacity to listen to patients' experience and imagine equally fulfilling ways of living that differ from our own. We cannot protect or do away with influences from society or our own lives in the clinical situation. Yet through our own awareness of these influences, inspection of our own and our patient's presumptions about couples, and willingness to be educated by our patients, we can maximize our capacity for identifying and entertaining new ways for people to conceptualize, assess, and potentially feel satisfied with their chosen relationships, however they might be configured, however they might be gendered.

References

Alexander, R. & Van Der Heide, N. P. (1997), Rage and aggression in couples therapy: An intersubjective approach. In: *Countertransference in Couples Therapy,* ed. M. F. Solomon & J. P. Siegel. New York: W. W. Norton, pp. 238–250.

Bacal, H. (1998), *Optimal Responsiveness: How Therapists Heal Their Patients.* Northvale, NJ: Aronson.

Benjamin, J. (1995), *Like Subjects, Love Objects: Essays on Recognition and Sexual Difference.* New Haven, CT: Yale University Press.

Brown, L. S. (1995), Therapy with same-sex couples: An introduction. In: *Clinical Handbook of Couple Therapy,* ed. N. S. Jacobson & A. S Gurman. New York: Guilford Press, pp. 274–291.

Cabaj, R. P. & Klinger, R. L. (1996), Psychotherapeutic interventions with lesbian and gay couples. In: *Textbook of Homosexuality and Mental Health,* ed. R. P. Cabaj & T. S. Stein. Washington, DC: American Psychiatric Press, pp. 485–501.

Fisher, S. K. (1993), A proposed Adlerian theoretical framework and intervention techniques for gay and lesbian couples: Individual Psychology. *J. Adlerian Theory, Res. & Practice,* 49:438–449.

Forstein, M. (1994), Psychotherapy with gay male couples: Loving in the time of AIDS. In: *Therapists on the Front Line: Psychotherapy with Gay Men in the Age of AIDS,* ed. S. A. Cadwell & R. A. Burnham, Jr. Washington, DC: American Psychiatric Press, pp. 293–315.

Freedman, E. (1996), Psychoanalysis and the world of two: Object relations couple therapy. In: *Fostering Healing and Growth: A Psychoanalytic Social Work Approach,* ed. J. Edward & J. B. Sanville. Northvale, NJ: Aronson, pp. 327–352.

Gerson, M. (1996), *The Embedded Self: A Psychoanalytic Guide to Family Therapy.* Hillsdale, NJ: The Analytic Press.

Gray, D. & Isensee, R. (1996), Balancing autonomy and intimacy in lesbian and gay relationships. In: *Gay and Lesbian Mental Health: A Sourcebook for Practitioners,* ed. C. J. Alexander. New York: Harrington Park Press/Haworth Press, pp. 95–114.

MacDonald, B. J. (1998), Issues in therapy with gay and lesbian couples. *J. Sex & Marital Ther.,* 24:165–190.

McMahon, M. (1997), Creating harmony out of dissonance Applying theories of intersubjectivity to therapy with couples. *J. Analytic Soc. Work,* 4:43–61.

Orange, D., Atwood, G. & Stolorow, R. (1997), *Working Intersubjectively: Contextualism in Psychoanalytic Practice.* Hillsdale, NJ: The Analytic Press.

Ringstrom, P. A. (1994), An intersubjective approach to conjoint therapy. In: *A Decade of Progress: Progress in Self Psychology, Vol. 10,* ed. A. Goldberg. Hillsdale, NJ: The Analytic Press, pp. 159–182.

Sander, F. M. (1998), Psychoanalytic couple therapy. In: *Case Studies in Couple and Family Therapy: Systemic and Cognitive Perspectives,* ed. F. M. Dattilio. New York: Guilford Press, pp. 427–449.

Simon, G. (1996), Working with people in relationships. In: *Pink Therapy: A Guide for Counselors and Therapists Working with Lesbian, Gay and Bisexual Clients,* ed. D. Davies & C. Neal. Buckingham, UK: Open University Press, pp. 101–115.

Singer, A. (1995), Gestalt couples therapy with gay male couples: Enlarging the therapeutic ground awareness. In: *On Intimate Ground: A Gestalt Approach to Working with Couples,* ed. G. Wheeler & S. Backman. San Francisco, CA: Jossey-Bass, pp. 166–187.

Stern, D. (1985), *The Interpersonal World of the Infant.* New York: Basic Books.

Stolorow, R. & Atwood, G. (1992), *Contexts of Being: The Intersubjective Foundations of Psychological Life.* Hillsdale, NJ: The Analytic Press.

————— ————— & Orange, D. (1999), Kohut and contextualism: Toward a post-Cartesian psychoanalytic theory. *Psychoanal. Psychol.,* 16:380–388.

————— Brandchaft, B. & Atwood, G. (1987), *Psychoanalytic Treatment: An Intersubjective Approach.* Hillsdale, NJ: The Analytic Press.

————— Orange, D. & Atwood, G. (1999), Toward post-Cartesian psychoanalytic theory: Commentary on paper by Bruce E. Reis. *Psychoanal. Dial.,* 9:401–406.

Trop, J. L. (1994), Conjoint therapy: An intersubjective approach. In: *A Decade of Progress: Progress in Self Psychology, Vol. 10,* ed. A. Goldberg. Hillsdale, NJ: The Analytic Press, pp. 147–158.

————— (1997), An intersubjective perspective of countertransference in couples therapy. In: *Countertransference in Couples*

Therapy, ed. M. F. Solomon & J. P. Siegel. New York: W. W. Norton, pp. 99–109.

Walsh, F. (1996), Partner abuse. In: *Pink therapy: A Guide for Counselors and Therapists Working with Lesbian, Gay and Bisexual Clients,* ed. D. Davies & C. Neal. Buckingham, UK: Open University Press, pp. 188–198.

4

The Interplay of Difference and Shame

Ann D'Ercole

I n individual therapy, there is an implicit agreement that the
therapist is on the side of the patient. In couple's therapy,
however, the therapist is on the side of the relationship.
This may leave each individual's vulnerabilities fully exposed to
his or her significant other. Given this reality, it inevitably takes
courage to invite a stranger, albeit a good-intentioned one, into
the intimate workings of a couple's private life. For lesbian and
gay couples seeking treatment, this invitation may present
greater hazards than those taken by their heterosexual cohorts.
Historically, because psychoanalytic practitioners obscured the
lives of lesbian and gay individuals in the language of patholo-
gy, immaturity, and immorality, psychoanalytic theorizing
about same-sex couples rarely went beyond judging them as
unworkable.

Toward the end of the 20th century, however, psychoanalysts
began reappraising their theory and treatment of lesbian and gay
individuals and couples. Those reappraisals have engaged clinicians in discussions that focus on understanding how lesbian and
gay identities are lived and articulated (O'Connor and Ryan, 1994;
Domenici and Lesser, 1995; Magee and Miller, 1997; Glazer and
Drescher, 2001; Kiersky and Gould, 2001; Drescher, D'Ercole, and
Schoenberg, 2003). Gay-affirmative clinicians have illustrated

how cultural messages can hinder intimacy for couples by creating barriers in an otherwise functioning relationship (Drescher, 1998). Nevertheless, mainstream psychoanalysis still lacks normative models for understanding the interpersonal dynamics of gay and lesbian couples. One aim of this chapter is to begin the process of correcting that omission.

For all couples, the intimate give and take of a relationship includes the complex configuration of cultural beliefs about attachment and autonomy. These cultural premises offer vague guidelines about how each partner should attain a relief from loneliness and a gratification of the yearning for affection and love. For example, we are told from the earliest age that girls marry boys and boys marry girls and that love is defined by these matchings. In that way, instructions on how connected — indeed intertwined — we may become and with whom are conveyed through a complex mixing of gender and sexuality with attachment and autonomy. Culture powerfully shapes day-to-day experiences of establishing and managing interdependence and mutuality in the context of a shared life. Couples therapy can provide an opportunity to deconstruct, reshape, and reconfigure those elements. It can bring into our expectations and focus a myriad of internal and external forces that guide, support, and define a couple's life. This can include body language, mood states, and nonverbal messages — both clear and ambiguous.

My basic approach toward therapy with same-sex couples is no different from my approach to treating heterosexual ones. It requires that the therapist enter into the family drama to reframe and clarify the idiosyncrasies of the relationship system. The therapist's ultimate purpose in participating in the relationship is to change it. This process requires that the therapist keep in mind some distinct difficulties that a same-sex couple can encounter as the two people establish a household, divide up domestic labor, and create a pattern of living without social and legal support.

For gay and lesbian couples, many situations can arise that lead them to question their basic existence and challenge their shared life. They may take the form of questions about domestic partnership, commitment ceremonies, or adopting or birthing children. Other questions arise around health care decisions for dying or disabled life partners, replacing biological family members as heirs, and acquiring family health care entitlements in the workplace. Same-sex couples may question how families of origin fit into their lives, their places of employment, and their social networks. These issues are further complicated by whether the two of them are accepted and acknowledged as a couple, by how they view themselves, and by how they represent themselves to the external world. For some couples, a resurgence of internalized shame can reappear when they contemplate having a family. They can find themselves faced with new tensions or pressures to resolve unconscious issues related to becoming a parent (Crespi, 2001).

The issue of difference also affects gay and lesbian couples. Over the years, I have become very attentive when the word "different" arises in therapy with a same-sex couple. While part of being human includes wanting to be appreciated for one's uniqueness, individuality, or differences, many people are afraid that being different means one is weird, pathological, or even perverted. For some, being different can be a source of pride or a trigger to envy (Morrison, 1996), but those who know their lives differ from heterosexual norms can experience wounding shame. In clinical experience with gay and lesbian patients, feelings of difference are often closely linked to feelings of shame. The recognition that one has failed to act in accordance with societal norms can often arouse shameful feelings, whether or not one accepts those norms as legitimate (Lewis, 1987; D'Ercole, 1996). For lesbian and gay couples, feelings of shame can be woven into the intricate tapestry of their relationships as it is embedded in subtle levels of interpersonal discourse and experience.

One benefit of couples therapy is that both people have an opportunity to share shameful and other feelings both to and with each other (Gerson, 2001). In an intense way, the ways in which they each shape and organize each other's experiences can become the basis for connection and a redefinition of selfhood. How these elements come together in the process of couples treatment is of course difficult to capture, and like all psychotherapy narratives, subject to revision. In describing a few sessions with a couple, this chapter tries to provide a glimpse into how feeling different can obscure shameful feelings, and how that shame can infiltrate and contaminate a relationship.

The Presenting Complaint

Dee came home one evening to find Susan entwined in the arms of another woman. It was a shocking and painful encounter for both of them, and they came to couples therapy almost immediately. Susan and Dee were each deeply troubled by the state of their relationship, but for different reasons. In fact, "different" was a defining element of how they saw themselves and one of the defining themes of our first sessions. They seemed to shape and organize their experiences by defining themselves as different — different from each other.

Dee and Susan came from opposite ends of the country, with distinct cultural backgrounds. Susan, older than Dee, saw their age difference as their greatest disparity. Dee, however, saw their differences more broadly. She saw Susan as flighty and herself as stoic. Dee understood this difference as cultural and it was far more important to her. They began their marriage four years before with a commitment ceremony and described the early part of their relationship as passionate and fun — a time when they were both busy but also enjoyed lots of time together.

Although they disagreed about almost everything, Susan and Dee did agree that their relationship changed when Dee went back to school two years earlier. At that time, Susan bitterly opposed Dee's decision to change careers, fearing it meant they would have much less time together. She openly accused Dee of being selfish and single-minded and felt Dee was indifferent to her objections. Over time, though Susan was outwardly resigned to accepting what Dee wanted, she maintained an internal accounting system in which Susan was the one who continually came up short. Susan secretly felt selfish for voicing her objections at all. Dee, on the other hand, plodded along her own path, ignoring as best she could Susan's unhappiness and attending only to the occasions when they enjoyed each other's company. Dee was adept at screening out all the difficult times by burying herself in her work. Eventually, Susan broke through Dee's withdrawal in a very loud way: a brief affair. In their first couples therapy session they both expressed doubts, with great sadness, that their relationship could be mended.

The Couple

Susan was a southern Baptist. Her parents met at a church function and married soon after. Mom stayed home, opting for full-time motherhood. Susan described her mother as a gentle tyrant with a "Pollyanna" veneer who devoted herself to home decoration and community work. Her Dad's work allowed him to be home early each evening. Following dinner, however, he would withdraw into the newspaper for hours or work in his basement workshop. Susan's one sibling, an older sister, was one of her closest friends. Her parents and sister agree that Susan was the star of the family. She took every extracurricular class and was expected to perform and shine. Susan thought their lives were perfect: No one ever quarreled and the family members had everything they needed, both materially and emotionally, within their tight-knit community. She summed it up in her playfully sarcastic way by saying, "My mother and father are wonderful parents. Always willing to help me. No one in my family ever fights. They just do what my mother wants and it's all fine." In many ways, Susan still appeared to be living in her family of origin.

Dee was brought up with six older siblings by a single mom who worked night and day to make ends meet. Her parents divorced early in Dee's life, and she described her family as a busy place where everyone took care of themselves. Her mother was busy working and keeping the house functioning. Dee saw her mother as frugal and hardworking, a no-nonsense kind of woman who ran a laissez-faire household where everyone was expected to do what was right. Only Dee seemed to have figured out what that was. Her siblings are less educated and ambitious. Dee described her father as stingy, unemotional, and uneducated but resourceful and extremely hardworking. Following the divorce, her father took a peripheral position in the family. Growing up, Dee felt no one in her family had time to talk. To Dee, action was what family was about.

Susan and Dee not only experienced their differences as an immovable object, it was like a wall they could neither traverse nor break down. When things went well for them, they did not experience this difference as a tension. But when life was hard, they each felt hopeless and helpless in the face of their differences. Both saw their futures in terms of their pasts. Susan felt that her own recent individual therapy had helped her to understand some of her feelings. She felt that, in her childhood, she had learned compliance rather than mediation, adaptation rather than self-articulation. She did not want to spend the rest of her life trying to please her mother.

Dee felt she had gotten the best she could from her individual therapy and wanted to focus on her relationship. She was overwhelmed by her current feelings of hurt and anger. She felt unappreciated and unacknowledged by Susan and feared that she would have to make a life on her own as her mother had done.

This couple seemed to be unaware of themselves in profound ways. Each of them needed to find a way to see who they were and whom they were with. That meant understanding the complexity of the other's individuality, including their gay identities. Despite the fact that Susan and Dee were outwardly open and accepting of their lesbian identities, they each held back a part of themselves from other people. They lived a selectively open life that allowed them a close circle of friends and acquaintances. Susan's parents were cordial to Dee, but far from welcoming. This left Dee feeling alienated from Susan who felt like she had failed both her parents and Dee. Dee's parents appeared less problematic, but also less demanding of Dee in general, and she was selective in revealing her relationship to colleagues. Dee and Susan live as do many gay and lesbian couples surrounded by a close network of friends who are supportive, reluctantly supportive family members who are less involved, and work colleagues who have little to do with the couple's joint life.

Beginning Treatment

In the beginning phase of the treatment, I expressed the opinion that a marital affair is often a symptom of preexisting problems in the relationship. I asked them if they felt that might be true, and they acknowledged that they had had some problems. Dee demanded to know why Susan had the affair. She was confused, but worse, she felt that Susan was not really sorry about causing her such pain. Susan felt that she had apologized and that there was nothing more she could do. Susan could not explain why it happened, beyond her sense of feeling lonely and abandoned by Dee. As it turns out, they had had this argument before, and it felt like an irresolvable circular narrative. Susan would express the fear that her only escape from the dreadful guilt she experienced was to leave the relationship. Dee would respond with more anger, accusing Susan of indulging her own feelings rather than trying to understand why she acted in the way she did or convincingly communicating real remorse.

The initial sessions were spent with Dee accusing Susan of withholding her feelings and Susan feeling angry and not heard. During these sessions, they would often leave the office in a storm of icy rage. At those times, I would be left thinking I might never see them again. Perhaps reflecting my own ambivalence, in some ways I hoped that would be true. There was a silent brutality to the way they fought. I thought that my frustration stemmed from my own feeling of being locked out. It was this feeling that I used to engage them, asking them to consider that perhaps that was how each of them felt. I further suggested that perhaps the affair was a way for Susan to capture Dee's attention. To Dee, I suggested that Susan's actions had essentially awakened her and asked her to consider why Susan might have to resort to such extremes to reach her. This inquiry seemed to move the discussion to new ground. In the questions, Susan heard that perhaps the fault in the relationship was not all hers. Dee heard it as a possible explanation for their difficulties, one in which she might be involved. She was willing to consider the possibility that Susan was trying to get her attention. We talked about what had happened in each of their families that may have led to this kind of lock out in their relationship.

Susan came to understand and was able to express how she felt betrayed by Dee. She experienced Dee's decision to return to school as abandonment and she could not bear the pain of her loss. She yearned to have Dee at home when she arrived from work, to have weekends free to play and enough money to enjoy all the things she had grown fond of doing. Dee had assured her it would only be a short time until they could resume their lives together. But Dee's previous attempts to minimize the impact of her absence from home were often met with a blank smile and sullen, icy hostility. Dee felt Susan could not appreciate the importance of Dee's new work. What's more, while Dee doggedly pursed her new career she also lobbied Susan to start a family. Dee felt time was running out because of her age, and she was unwilling to give up the wish and their earlier agreement that they would have a family. The issue of starting a family emerged openly in the treatment at about this point, but it had been a quiet background issue for this couple throughout their relationship. At this point, Susan felt unduly pressured to agree to parenthood and reexperienced her fears of abandonment or of being replaced in Dee's heart. Dee felt Susan's opposition as that of a withholding parent or — even worse — a jealous mother who wished to deny her daughter's fertility. Her investment in having a child seemed so great that she was unable to consider the serious objections Susan raised.

In listening to the way they described their experiences, I thought about the unconscious pressures Susan and Dee felt to construct their particular sense of couplehood. They both found ways to reconstruct what they had experienced in their families of origin. Susan, for example, reconstructed her sense of being controlled by her mother. She felt she had to do everything Dee wanted: accept Dee's career change and start a family. To stay connected, she had to accept everything on Dee's terms. Dee, on the other hand, felt locked out of Susan's feeling world and, like her single mother, feared she would be left having to do everything herself. She worried that she might have to choose between her partner and her wish to have a child.

Treatment Deepens
Susan and Dee approached their life together with a predetermined blueprint, one that was fixed and unchanging. In our work, I introduced the notion that a blueprint could make room for contingency and choice (Hoffman, 2000). Susan and Dee had built a life that suited them both in many ways. When not engaged in their anger, Susan and Dee were eager to talk about

themselves and were engaging. Over time, I found myself thinking I was having too good a time. I laughed at their jokes and
looked forward to our meetings. I noticed that they were both
flirting with me and that I seemed to enjoy it. It certainly was a
pleasant relief from the earlier brutality, and it did not seem to
be a defense against our mutual efforts.

I shared my feelings with them and asked if either of them
experienced what I described. Not only did they understand
how I felt, but they also had been talking about it between our
meetings. Susan let me know how they talk about which of
them I preferred. Each of them felt I preferred the other. They
seemed to be showing me a side of themselves they had withdrawn from one another. The domestic war had been suspend-
ed within our sessions and they had begun to reengage in a
playful intimacy that had marked their early relationship. In
some ways, I felt let inside a circle of intimacy in which the
shame that permeated the beginning of treatment was absent. I
was a witness to their deconstruction of separateness and their
acceptance of connection from which emerged an extremely
important revelation. Susan seemed to be actively engaged in
understanding how Dee's orientation to action challenged
Susan's tendency to try and keep things from changing. Dee
was more concerned with what she called "getting things done"
and less concerned with examining the attendant feelings. Dee's
approach left Susan feeling that there was little time for her to
express or even understand what she felt

I also considered my own participation. Their playful "flirting"
with me seemed to provide a space that confirmed the connection
between excitement and uncertainty, making uncertainty possible
by making it exciting (Phillips, 1994, p. 12). This atmosphere of
uncertainty and excitement seems to provide a sense of safety in
the therapeutic relationship, which allowed Susan and Dee to
reexperience each other. I found Dee and Susan to be equally interesting, intelligent, and attractive women. Perhaps my willingness
to tease and be teased reflected a sense of acceptance of their feelings — a positive mirroring of their emotional and erotic experiences to counter the feelings of shame. Of course, my feeling that
I may have been enjoying it *too much* suggests that I also carried
some of the uncertainty, guilt, and shame.

In this middle phase of the treatment, Susan and Dee began to make changes in the structure of their lives outside the session. A threatened loss of a beloved house brought on a resurgence of their earlier inability to empathize with one another. As they struggled with their feelings about the house, I wondered if they each could sympathize with her partner's internal struggles rather than become angry and attacking. It seemed to me that only with the establishment of mutual empathy could they begin to hear and consider each other's concerns about their relationship, family, and individual lives.

I asked Dee if, rather than stonewalling her feelings, she could empathize with Susan's fear that she would not survive her failure to get what she most wanted. Dee thought about it and described how growing up, she knew her mother did not have time or emotional energy to comfort her, so she kept herself directed forward, cultivating a form of will in the face of deprivation, loss, and neglect. This defensive approach to her feelings blocked Dee's ability to join with Susan or to offer her comfort around the impending loss of the home they both wanted.

In their sessions, Susan and Dee actively engaged in reconstructing their life stories together. They would take a few painful steps forward and then revert back to their self-protective positions. They were tangled in misunderstandings and in their fantasized versions of their relationship. Dee's fantasy relationship was one that had Susan embracing optimism risk. They could have a baby, buy a new house, and still have time for each other. She would have the longed-for partner who was fully and equally engaged, beloved by her spouse, and committed to raising a family. Feeling increasingly anxious and hopeless about the widening gulf between her hoped-for and lived experience, Dee became accusatory as she sought an explanation to Susan's objections. This, in turn, increased Susan's anxiety, preventing her from helping Dee understand the factors that precluded the hoped-for experience. Unable to see this, and faced with Susan's defensiveness, Dee experienced Susan as unresponsive, uncaring, and ultimately responsible for her unhappiness. Afraid she would further alienate Dee, Susan retreated to silence. Susan's fantasy life imagined Dee concerned with and attentive to her worries. In her silence, Susan imagined a perfect mate. A fantasized other who would attend to her worries and not insist she move forward. This perfect mate would embrace her concerns and stand by her side.

Final Phase of Treatment

In the final phase of treatment, it seemed that the more things improved for Susan and Dee outside of our sessions, the more difficult the sessions became. Dee opened up the discussion. "You can't be with us all the time; we have to figure this out without you." I agreed with her and wondered if I had become too much a member of the family. Susan took a different tack. She became more direct, explaining to Dee that she was used to being the center of attention both in her family and at work. She felt that they had worked on this issue in our sessions and that it had improved, but that it was still difficult for her not to have Dee's attention. Dee and Susan described how they still kept the most dangerous issues at bay and avoided talking about anything disturbing. In fact, when coming to a session, Susan still found herself trying not to upset Dee to avoid having to deal with her later. Dee found this disclosure important because she felt she welcomed Susan's concerns and wanted to deal with them head on, rather than live locked out of Susan's subjective experience. Susan also wanted more physical intimacy. She wanted to feel wanted. Bravely, she asked Dee to touch her more often, to offer her affection. Dee explained to Susan how important talking and sharing were to her. She felt if they talked more, there would be more sexual intimacy as well.

Slowly, they revealed their fears, and dissatisfactions. The pleasures of their domestic life replaced the circular, affect-laden arguments. Susan feared that Dee would leave her if she did not do things her way, much as her mother threatened to withdraw her love if things were not done her way. Dee felt doomed to live her life without talking or touching — just as she had in her family of origin. She had reconstructed a busy but cold environment. She wanted to have a family, and Susan put up roadblocks instead of solutions. Those roadblocks turned out to hide a deeply felt shame, a sense of "wrongness" and "deviance" buried in old self-concepts and convictions that needed careful, empathic attention and therapeutic work.

In the course of the treatment, Susan and Dee explored the interplay between feeling different and feelings of shame. Over time, it seemed that one feeling was tucked inside the other, standing in for, then replacing the other. For example, Susan felt she was too old to become a mother. She would be too different — different from Dee, but also different from other mothers. Her subjective experience of difference seemed to be a defense against the more painful feelings of shame.

Susan brought a dream into a session. "I see you Dee holding this little kid's hand and you won't let me into where you are going. And it felt rotten." The context of this dream is important. Susan is telling her dream to her partner and her therapist during a joint therapy session. In this instance, the interpretation of Susan's felt experience of "rotten" was recognized, as was her hope that she might forge a connection and her continuing fear that she would be excluded from that connection. Her feeling rotten, decayed, corrupt, possibly immoral related to Susan's experience of feeling different and how that difference would exclude her from the future she wanted. The dream underscored Susan's wish to be included in something loving and close — to join Dee as she goes forward with a child. In contrast, the feelings of exclusion were palpable.

It emerged that Susan's mother had demanded a complete devotion and tended to block Susan from other substantive relationships, thus forcing on her child a guilt-ridden conflict of loyalty. By focusing on the social aspects of the dream, Susan explored what felt decayed, unhealthy, perhaps crazy, or vulgar to her. Susan wanted to be connected and to move forward feeling complete and nourished. In the analysis of this dream, Susan spoke openly about her fears of being part of a two-mom family. Susan thought she gave up that possibility long ago, as women of her generation did not see motherhood as an option for lesbian couples. This idea was linked with her feelings about her age. She was ostensibly saying she was too old to become a mother, but she was also speaking about the shame of being beyond childbearing years as well as the shame of being a lesbian mom. She explained to Dee how she feared she could not keep their relationship hidden from work colleagues once they had a child. She was afraid to tell her parents. The way she lived her life would become obvious to everyone.

Susan began to see her concerns about her age as a substitute for her concerns about being perceived as different. Shame seemed to emerge as the ever-present obstacle to Susan and Dee's ability to grow together. Dee worried that Susan would be unable to move on, and Susan was concerned she would be locked out of a future with Dee. The dream provided an opportunity for Susan and Dee to build a mutual understanding of where they were and where they had been.

On Difference

In this relationship there was an intense interplay between difference and shame. It was part of the dialogue of Susan and Dee's relationship, sometimes appearing as feelings of shame, other times as feeling different. The issue of shame about being different was not immediately apparent, but was instead obscured by other issues such as feeling shameful about an affair, feeling ashamed of the desire to have a family past the "appropriate age," and feeling different because of that desire. Susan and Dee came to see how their childhood worlds were, in fact, similar as well as different. Both Susan and Dee feared that revealing their private experiences of shame posed a threat to their connection. In the couple's treatment, a world was created in which Susan and Dee were invited to talk about and explore their experiences while remaining connected. They explored how they relied on one another's differences and how the very notion of difference carried complex meanings — including meanings of shame. While the problems Susan and Dee brought into treatment did not evaporate, with the lessening of shame, the shift in their relatedness seemed firm and enduring.

References

Crespi, L. (2001), And baby makes three: A dynamic look at development and conflict in lesbian families. *J. Gay & Lesbian Psychother.*, 4(3/4):7–29.

D'Ercole, A. (1996), Designing the lesbian subject: Looking backwards — looking forwards. In: *That Obscure Subject of Desire: Freud's Female Homosexual Revisited*, ed. R. Lesser & E. Schoenberg. New York: Routledge, pp. 115–129.

Domenici, T. & Lesser, R., eds. (1995), *Disorienting Sexuality: Psychoanalytic Reappraisals of Sexual Identities*. New York: Routledge.

Drescher, J. (1998), *Psychoanalytic Therapy and the Gay Man*. Hillsdale, NJ: The Analytic Press, 2001.

———— D'Ercole, A. & Schoenberg, E., eds. (2003), *Psychotherapy with Gay Men and Lesbians: Contemporary Dynamic Approaches*. Binghamton, NY: Harrington Park Press.

Gerson, M. J. (2001), The ritual of couples therapy: The subversion of autonomy. *Contemp. Psychoanal.*, 37:453–470.

Glazer, D. F. & Drescher, J., eds. (2001), *Gay and Lesbian Parenting*. New York: Haworth Press.

Gould, E. & Kiersky, S., eds. (2001), *Sexualities Lost and Found: Lesbians, Psychoanalysis, and Culture*. Madison, CT: International Universities Press.

Hoffman, I. (2000), At death's door: Therapists and patients as agents. *Psychoanal. Dial.*, 10:823–846.

Lewis, H. B., ed. (1987), *The Role of Shame in Symptom Formation*. Mahwah, NJ: Lawrence Erlbaum Associates.

Magee, M. & Miller, D. (1997), *Lesbian Lives: Psychoanalytic Narratives Old and New*. Hillsdale, NJ: The Analytic Press.

Morrison, A. (1996), *The Culture of Shame*. New York: Ballantine.

O'Connor, N. & Ryan, J. (1994), *Wild Desires and Mistaken Identities: Lesbianism and Psychoanalysis*. New York: Columbia University Press.

Phillips, A. (1994), *On Flirtation*. Cambridge, MA: Harvard University Press.

5

"Is This Normal?"
Uncovering the Role of Homophobia in the Treatment of a Lesbian Couple

Judy A. Levitz

W orking with couples can be one of the most challenging and rewarding experiences in psychoanalytic work. In treating same-sex couples, one generally finds that the presenting issues do not differ notably from those presented by heterosexual couples. Typically, problems derive from communication difficulties, power imbalances, conflicts engendered by different characterological styles, and ultimately from transference enactments and projections. One notable difference is the role of internalized homophobia as it affects the couple's dynamics. Recent psychoanalytic writings emphasize the importance of recognizing the impact of every level of cultural homophobia that traumatically or insidiously complicate the development of a healthy self (Drescher, 1998). In couples' treatment, manifestations of unresolved homophobic feelings often underlie or are obscured by other conflicts, thereby adding an additional layer of resistance to improved interaction. An example of this is a case in which the intense intellectual competitiveness of one partner resulted in the other partner feeling constantly devalued. When explored more deeply, the competitive trait was found to be linked with an unconscious drive to compensate for underlying feelings of inadequacy related to sexual orientation.

This chapter uses a case illustration of a couple in which both partners had deep-seated problems relating to different aspects of their sexuality. For one, the return of repressed homophobic feelings appeared in countless disguises; for the other, reliance on dissociative defenses to keep memories of childhood sexual abuse at bay played a major role in her interactions. The primary obstacle to moving the work forward was the camouflaged homophobia, and thus this occupies center stage in this chapter. Some attention is given to the role of sexual abuse trauma on the relationship, as well.

A Theoretical Survival Kit
Before describing the case itself, I briefly bookmark the primary concepts that generally inform my work with couples. This "theoretical survival kit" keeps me afloat despite the powerful transferences and enactments that threaten to drown the couple, the therapist, and the treatment itself. With judicious use and integration of a broad range of analytic and systems interventions (Ackerman, 1966; Stierlin, 1977; Scharff and Scharff, 1991), most couples work can proceed along a predictable and familiar course of development and resolution. Systems goals usually center on improving communications and require that each member understand his or her role in the system, its impact on the other person, and how interchanges are perceived or received. Analytic goals emphasize something slightly different in couples therapy — namely, the need to resolve each partner's resistance to the interpersonal changes. This requires more sustained and in-depth uncovering of earlier patterns and their repetitions and enactments. With this as a backdrop to the work, three phases of the relationship during which different transference states tend to infuse the day-to-day interactions are presented: (a) The *honeymoon phase* in which the partners share the experience of a mutual idealized transference to each other, (b) the *phase of disillusionment* in which the negative transference reactions to each other manifest, and (c) the *phase of realistic integration* in which an acceptance or resolution of obstacles that stand in the way of the more integrated, mature way of relating has been achieved. It is within this overarching paradigm (which is further described later) that four key concepts derived from self psychol-

ogy, drive and ego psychology, and object relational models are applied. They are the notion of selfobject, the negative narcissistic transference, role expectations, and projective identification.

The Selfobject Functioning of the Partners

The Kohutian concept of the selfobject as applied to the selfobject functioning of partners facilitates the understanding of intimate dyadic interactions (Kohut, 1971; Epstein and Feiner, 1979). Couples routinely provide each other with mirroring validation that spans a vast range of nonpathological interdependency. For example, one member of the couple may be the calming force in the face of anxiety; another may serve as the couple's social conduit. This extends beyond the more obvious interactions to those that pertain to the stabilizing but imperceptible physical and emotional feedback that provides a core validation of the other's observations, beliefs, behaviors, and so on.

The Negative Narcissistic Transference

This concept is drawn from Modern Analytic theory (Spotnitz, 1969) and refers to early positive and negative transferences deriving from the preoedipal stage of development. Of course it is the negative ones that present the greatest obstacles to therapeutic change. Unconscious projections and entanglements manifest in the communications through expressions of unconstructive anger or blaming, withdrawal from the partner, depression, self-attack, passivity, acting out, somatization, and so on (Margolis, 1994). The work of the therapist is to help the partners be aware of these narcissistic transference components by increasing their awareness of expectations and differences, gradually moving each person into a more reality-based position vis-à-vis the other.

Role Expectations

The three-phase model described earlier contains shorthand descriptions of a couple traveling through stages of relating that incorporate what Sandler and Sandler (1978) refer to as *role expectations*. This object relational tool is another crucial guidepost to helping the therapist identify the nature of the transference that occupies the foreground at any given time:

In the honeymoon period, when the idealizing transference drives the relationship, the partner is perceived to have all the qualities suited for effortlessly meeting the needs of the other. It primarily occurs in the falling-in-love stage and is accompanied by the fantasy (which is experienced as an excited reality) that the similar attitudes, interests, and values of the lover will validate and elevate the uniqueness of the self. Even opposite character traits are perceived as desirable and admirable, and unconsciously viewed as conduits into aspects of the world that the individual alone was not able to access. The expectation is that "I am known," that is "I don't have to ask," "I don't have to say," "she [he] knows," and so on. It is usually after the idealized transferences have yielded to negative transferences due to the inevitable regressions that occur in intimate relationships that the couple comes for help.

In the phase of disillusionment in which the negative narcissistic transference reigns, the expectation is "I shouldn't have to ask, say, she [he] should know, "and so on. The disappointments and frustrations from repeated failures are soon fueled by historical angers and betrayals. The work of the analyst here is to uncover the fundamental needs being defended and help the members of the couple articulate their expectations. Once this occurs, it becomes possible to separate the transference enactments from the real needs and expectations and help the couple communicate effectively about them. This enables the negative and narcissistic transferences to yield to the more realistic and mature level of relating.

In the reality integration phase of the relationship, each partner has been able to achieve an acceptance and understanding of the other's character, behavior, and needs. There is greater opportunity and capacity to interact with the real partner, as opposed to one partner's internalized self or parental objects, or one's internalized parental couple. The separateness attained protects the couple from overly extreme or destructive regressions.

Projective Identification
Finally, the work of using the couple's projective identifications is essential for ultimate resolution of resistances because it is the key to understanding the nuances of the unconscious processes

(Ogden, 1979). For example, couples often come to therapy with one partner fearing that the other is going to leave the relationship. This fear can turn into certainty, irritating the other to the point of her actually wanting to leave. What can emerge in the couples work is some fear or ambivalence in the first partner and how, through projective identification, she was able to rid herself of this unwanted feeling.

The clinical impact of internalized homophobia and the internalization of the antihomosexual culture are not always evident when a patient first presents (Drescher, 1998). This may be especially relevant when there is no overt conflict about one's sexual orientation, but rather some other disguised component, such as unresolved mourning of a heterosexual lifestyle that undermines fuller intimacy (Crespi, 1995). Similarly, a dissociated sense of shame, displaced or projected paranoia, or an eating disorder, to name a few, could be the consequence of adaptations to repeated traumatic inscriptions (Cole, 2002). For couples in a committed relationship, it may be more difficult for the members to admit or, for that matter, to be completely conscious of their own internalized homophobia. For the therapist, it is also easy when working with such couples to find oneself looking elsewhere for explanations of what is at the core of the relational conflicts. In the case that follows, a unique confluence of the subterranean themes of internalized homophobia and childhood sexual trauma was uncovered as the work progressed beyond the resolution of the more manifest communication patterns, interpersonal conflicts, role expectations, and selfobject functioning between the partners.

Case Vignette: Jean and Marietta

Phase One
Jean and Marietta are two successful professionals in the arts, both in their late 30s who came into couples therapy after four years of living together. Jean had become extremely distraught over Marietta's reaction to the idea of adopting a child. Jean had struggled with this decision for a long time in individual therapy, and when she first presented it to Marietta, Marietta's response was, "If it's important to you, I'll do it." Jean reacted

by becoming a mixture of enraged, despondent, and severely anxious, because she expected a much more enthusiastic response. At her therapist's suggestion, they decided to enter couples therapy.

During the initial session, Jean and Marietta sat close, bodies touching on the couch, while Jean alternately took Marietta's hand or put an arm around her. Jean, a bright, nervous woman usually spoke first. She alternated between demeaning herself with self-attacking jokes and leveling sarcastic, critical jibes at Marietta. Marietta, who seemed passively sweet and a little depressed, was usually the responder. She listened to Jean's "lighthearted" attacks of her through a quietly thoughtful and slightly withdrawn posture. She seemed bent on keeping the peace.

In this early phase of treatment, I tried to assess the developmental level of the couple (i.e., how self-focused versus object-related the partners are) by noting things such as whether one partner looked away while the other spoke; if they corrected each other or there was only one-way correction; what kind of space was allowed for different perceptions and understandings, and so on. I noted Jean and Marietta's presenting character styles, their main mode of communicating, and discerned their manifest roles. Jean took the lead speaking and led the affectionate display. Marietta deferred to Jean, but the subtle presence or absence of Marietta's validating response powerfully affected Jean's subsequent reaction.

During the next two sessions, the issue of the adoption, or "the baby thing" as Jean called it, was the leading presenting problem. Although Jean continued to be affectionate, she couldn't speak without constantly looking over at Marietta to monitor her reactions. She was quick to backtrack or apologize if Marietta appeared at all confused, distressed or withdrawn. She tried with humor to make light of their difficulties and frequently said, "This is probably just normal stuff that all couples go through . . . right?"

I hypothesized that some version of Jean's dependency on Marietta was obscured by Jean's ostensible leadership role. Similarly, Marietta's power in the relationship was a bit clouded by her manifest passivity. Jean and Marietta's positive feelings led the way in this initial phase, and each partner put her best foot forward. But soon, the polite quipping and acquiescing yielded to the next level of conflict. Jean let a litany of complaints spill forth: "Marietta can't remember to close the garage door, she doesn't take responsibility for following up with the plumber, she never makes sure that the lawn is mowed when it's her turn, she can't be trusted to turn off the flame under the teapot before the water has boiled out."

Furthermore, Jean complained that Marietta never called when she was going to be home late, didn't consider asking Jean if it was all right to bring a friend home to dinner, and always left vacation planning and bill paying to Jean. Jean punctuated each charge on the list with the question, "Is this normal?"

Marietta innocently protested: "I didn't know these things bothered Jean quite as much as they do." Then she would add, "I'm glad she's telling me now."

For the most part, Marietta continued to validate Jean's rendition of the facts, admitted to being absentminded, and was apologetic for "spacing out." She promised to try harder to remember these things. Marietta had no complaints herself, just, "I wish Jean wouldn't get so angry."

Upon hearing this response, whatever good humor and ostensible tolerance Jean still mustered dissolved completely into exasperation and righteous indignation. Jean then brought the full weight of her angry and intensely critical feelings into the sessions, while Marietta more and more anxiously asserted that she can't take in what Jean wants when she yells and is so "mean."

Phase Two
As the expression of angry and critical feelings waxed and waned, there came hints of jealousy and fear of being left on the part of both partners. During a key period within this phase, Jean expressed anger at Marietta for not staying closer to her while they mingled at parties. Then, Marietta came into one session nervously revealing that Jean confessed to being physically drawn to a mutual friend of theirs that they saw often at social engagements. Jean assured Marietta that while she hadn't and wouldn't act on her feelings of attraction, it was certainly a consequence of

their unsatisfactory sexual relationship. Jean was terrified to talk about sex but angry to the point that I felt she wished her relationship with Marietta would fall apart so that she *could* sleep with another woman. Shortly on the heels of this, Marietta announced that she wanted to have more contact with her ex-lover. She insisted that she ought to be entitled to have a relationship with her despite the fact that it made Jean angry. "There is nothing sexual about it," she protested, so Jean should have nothing to fear. Interestingly, Marietta saw no connection between this and Jean's recent disclosure of her attraction to their friend. She seemed uncharacteristically rigid when it came to trying to discuss it in the sessions.

In the space of just over a month, these themes emerged as a part of the inevitable regression that hinted at the underlying transferences. It became necessary and possible to focus on an assessment of each partner's historical pattern that was shaped by the internalized individual parental introjects as well as the internalized parental couple roles. Interjecting questions about Jean and Marietta's parents strategically served to both cool the rapidly rising temperatures in the room and collect significant information that could move the treatment forward (Margolis, 1994).

Relevant Family Histories
Jean grew up with an ambivalently attached and narcissistic mother and a severely anxious and critical father. Jean described her father as both a hypochondriac and as someone who yelled a great deal and worried constantly. He perceived the world as totally unsafe and untrustworthy. Her mother usually withdrew and avoided saying or doing anything that would fan the flames of his outbursts. Mrs. J seemed to have been unable to effectively intervene in any way that might reassure Jean and her two younger sisters that the father was not really ill and that she could provide them with a buffer against his explosions. This influenced Jean's own tendency to experience a mild paranoia, taking the form of fears that everything would go wrong if she didn't control it. She felt she had to care for the caretakers who were overwhelmed by everything (internal and external). Having no model for internalizing a self-soothing object

(indeed, having internalized the anxiously attached object), she could never trust that she'd be safe in the world, and she harbored an intense wish, need, and expectation that Marietta would fulfill this role.

Marietta, a survivor of childhood sexual trauma at the hands of her father's brother, grew up in a household where her father was a depressed and controlling presence. Her mother was an unpredictable brew of ambivalent, passive, and intrusive. They had to care for Marietta's younger brother who was emotionally disturbed and was the focus of most of her parents' anxious attentions. She was expected to put aside her needs in deference to the brother and was taught to dismiss her frustrations and resentments because he "couldn't help" doing the things he did to annoy, hurt, scare, or overshadow her. She was taught to dismiss and forgive and appeared to learn this well. In fact, she had simply learned to perfect her ability to compartmentalize, dissociate, and deny. These characteristics became entrenched as she was more frequently dropped at her aunt and uncle's home and repeatedly molested by the uncle when they were upstairs watching television together.

In the first two phases of the treatment, a great deal of information had been collected: the selfobject functions that each partner served vis-à-vis the other, the role expectations that were both consciously and unconsciously held, the transference repetitions and enactments that unfolded in the regressive patterns of relating, and the defensive patterns that became entrenched by virtue of how these patterns interfaced with each other. These could be synthesized as follows:

(1) Jean was initially attracted to Marietta because of Marietta's veneer of calm, but this calm came to be experienced by Jean as passivity. Similarly, Marietta's lack of neediness later became identified as depression. "Marietta doesn't worry" became "Marietta doesn't remember anything — she's oblivious"; "Marietta's sociable and friendly" later became "Marietta lets anyone come into the house, and we have to take care of them."

(2) Marietta was attracted to Jean based on some conscious expectations of having a confident and capable caretaker who would keep her safe. Jean's competency became seen as controllingness, her attention to detailed matters was eventually

perceived as anxious obsessing, and her sexual initiative came to be experienced by Marietta as dominating and intrusive.

(3) Jean, who presented as the tougher and more in control partner, unconsciously endowed Marietta with the responsibility for relieving her anxiety (identification with the anxious father). Marietta was expected to dispel Jean's fears and relieve her ambivalence about most matters. There was a powerful expectation, first unconscious and later uncovered that if Marietta was strong and definitive, Jean could feel taken care of, protected, and absolved of the task of deciding how she herself felt (identification with the ambivalent mother). Hence, when Marietta reacted in a less than totally enthusiastic manner in response to the adoption idea, Jean's own ambivalence was not relieved. The selfobject function ascribed to Marietta was inadequately performed, leading to the classic rupture that unleashed her rage. The rage was both Jean's primary defense against anxiety and insecurity, but also, by expressing herself in a volatile, disorganized way, she made her contribution to the couple's immobilization in a primary transference repetition.

(4) Marietta's contribution was quite different. She gave Jean the role — both manifestly and unconsciously — of being the carrier of her (Marietta's) emotional intensity. Most importantly, Jean was meant to function as Marietta's memory, so that Marietta could keep her past from catching up to her. The enactment proceeded — and Marietta's narcissistic defenses (e.g., withdrawal, dissociation, etc.), which defended against unwanted feelings and vulnerabilities, were heightened. Marietta's detached passivity was self-protective, but Jean experienced this as abandoning and then reacted in a way that drove Marietta further away. Thus ensued the vicious cycle.

Under most circumstances, the therapist will see some of these patterns gradually dissolve and yield to more constructive interactions. This, of course, requires ongoing repetition of the enactments while the therapist first listens and tolerates, then explores and clarifies, joins and describes, and finally connects and interprets.

With Jean and Marietta however, such signs had not yet become evident nor were any significant changes in the communication patterns being sustained. When a treatment does not progress, the focus must shift to a closer scrutiny of the repetitions (Freud, 1914; Spotnitz, 1969). In couples work as well as in individual analysis, the repetition of anything — be it a phrase, an action, a dream, and so forth — is an opportunity to revisit an issue and know that somewhere imbedded in the repetition lies a clue to its resolution. The recurring arguments themselves did not give me the direction I needed. Ultimately, my attention was drawn to Jean's repeated question, "Is this normal?"

I began to notice the many forms the query took and how often it surfaced in different contexts. I hypothesized that Jean's identification with her father, specifically her fear of being 'crazy' like him, was a central unresolved intrapsychic issue that interfered with the progress of the couple's work. With that in mind, whenever some version of "Is this normal?" came up, I shifted from focusing on the comparisons of Jean's or Marietta's internalized parental couple with their "real" relationship (and untangling their expectations of how couples should relate based on past histories and personal fantasies of the ideal couple). I tried instead to explore more aspects of their individual identifications with each parental figure.

This enabled Jean to see the ways in which she was different from her father, and how, in the areas where she did behave similarly to him, her responses were triggered by neediness, rather than "meanness" or "craziness," as she feared. For a time, the focus on this aspect of Jean's internal structure seemed to pay off with a measurable decrease in her anxiety and anger. Once again, however, it did not seem to last or take hold in a way that shifted the couple interactions, and shortly afterward the interactions deteriorated into a period of cool tension, tenuousness, or heated fighting. It was right after this that Jean's fantasy of being sexual with her friend and Marietta's desire to be nonsexual with her former lover was first revealed. Jean was rather desperate in her wish to be reassured that both her attraction and her fury at Marietta for wanting to see her ex-lover were normal reactions. The "normality" theme resurfaced again and again:

Is it normal to be *this* angry and still think you can be with this person? Is it normal to be so oblivious not only to me but to your own safety? Is it normal to be attracted to someone else? Is it normal to accept not being more sexual?

Now I began formulate a different hypothesis. What if for
Jean, "Is *this* normal?" meant "Am *I* normal?" But not as I had
initially thought — "Am I normal" that is "not crazy" like my
father, but "Am I normal if I am not heterosexual like my parents?" At the same time, what if for Marietta, the question was,
"Do I want to reclaim my sexuality and experience my sexual
feelings? Can I protect myself if I do?"

Phase Three
From this point on, I considered the problem through another
lens. Beyond the manifest couple dynamics and imbedded role
conflicts, I focused on ways in which the collision of Jean's
unconscious homophobia and Marietta's unresolved sexual
abuse history influenced this couple's unique pattern of relating. In subsequent sessions, I attempted to reinterpret conflicts
in this light to see if I could gain traction in the treatment. At this
level of analytic awareness, new questions and formulations
could be considered and the work expanded.

For example, the initial trigger leading the couple into therapy was Marietta's response to Jean's desire to adopt a baby. As
noted by Glazer (1998, 2001), experiences relating to mothering
can reawaken fears of homophobia, and in Jean's case, it was the
stimulus that finally destroyed whatever homeostasis the relationship held. The other complaints which quickly replaced this
presenting problem were also understood differently; whereas
Jean had in the past furiously complained that Marietta had not
mowed the lawn and it was getting way out of hand, it now
emerged that the anger was a defense against a deeper anxiety
with a homophobic component. Exploring each of their feelings
about unruly grass, it predictably did not faze Marietta at all,
but it drew out new feelings from Jean. She first remarked that
it might hurt the property value. Then, she insisted that she'd be
embarrassed, and upon even further inquiry, she revealed that
she'd feel terribly exposed. They'd be "bringing attention to
themselves" and she didn't know if she could be "out" to her
neighbors. At best, the wild garden would invite people to
notice who lived there; at worst, it would justify the neighbors'
negative stereotype of lesbians.

In another session, Jean came in crying because Marietta said she had associations to being molested when Jean tried to make love to her over the weekend. Jean experienced this as a deep narcissistic injury and didn't know what to do. Marietta revealed she had become more aware that issues relating to past sexual abuse at the hands of her uncle sometimes surfaced and made her feel uncomfortable about having sex. She stated that while she could still enjoy it, she found herself getting depressed afterward. We began to work through more of Marietta's discomfort with her own anger and assertiveness which had been seriously blocking her from feeling she could adequately protect herself — not just from Jean's anger, as had previously been discussed, but from an unwanted sexual advance. We ultimately identified her withdrawal and forgetting as substitutes for direct confrontation and connected her dissociations to the original dissociative defenses that enabled her to disown her sexual feelings.

Systematically, the themes permeating their clashes were understood in a similar manner. Tables 1 and 2 outline examples of what first manifested as a complaint, was subsequently discussed in the context of interpersonal role expectations, and finally was integrated within the deeper context of their imbedded intrapsychic conflicts.

Finally, during this third phase of treatment, most of the issues that needed to be confronted and mourned for healthy integration and commitment in a relationship were now conscious enough to be addressed. Initially, Jean's reliance on Marietta to perform the selfobject function of mirroring and validation for her life choice was repeatedly "ruptured" by Marietta's inadequate responses. It was not only easier now for Jean both to own and to see the need to work through her own homophobic feelings, it was also possible for Jean and Marietta to talk together about how it felt being lesbians in their families, in their social network, and at their jobs.

Marietta's discomfort was not so centered about homosexuality per se as it was about sexuality in general. Not only did more overtly sexually relevant and identity-related material begin to emerge, it also could be discussed in a deeper way. Each of Jean's manifest complaints was redefined, as were the meaning of Marietta's defensive reactions. Her initial reliance

Table 1

Jean's Complaints, Conflicts, and Metacommunications

JEAN'S MANIFEST COMPLAINTS	LATENT ROLE and RELATIONAL CONFLICTS	JEAN'S UNCONSCIOUS HOMOPHOBIA
(Which emerged in the early negative phase.)	(Which were explored in the later negative phase.)	(Which was uncovered in the final working through phase.)
"Marietta never mows the lawn."	"She doesn't share responsibilities or follow through with things."	"What will people think if ours is the only messy garden?" *What will the neighbors think of these lesbians?*
"Marietta always forgets to close the garage door."	"Everything is up to me." "Marietta can't be relied upon to protect me."	"Somebody could break in or be hiding in the house." *As lesbians we are more vulnerable to attack.*
"Marietta should have been happier about adopting a baby."	"She's not truly committed to me."	"Why can't we be like everybody else?" *I'm with someone who is not helping me achieve more social sanctions as is possible in the heterosexual world.*
"Marietta never helps with vacation plans."	"Marietta is always leaving me all the work, and is not able to/willing to take care of me."	"I make all the arrangements all the time, I always have to be the one to call or ask for the queen instead of the 2 double beds." *I'm alone in coming out.*
"Marietta never really wants to have or initiate sex."	"She's always putting everyone and everything else first."	"She's not attracted to me." *No one is validating my sexuality.*

Table 2
Marietta's Complaints, Conflicts, and Metacommunications

MARIETTA'S MANIFEST COMPLAINTS	UNDERLYING ROLE and RELATIONAL CONFLICTS	MARIETTA'S UNCONSCIOUS SURVIVOR ISSUE
(Which emerged in the early negative phase.)	(Which were explored in the later negative phase.)	(Which was uncovered in the final working through phase.)
"I don't like when Jean yells at me."	"Jean doesn't respect me or consider my feelings."	*I feel abused when she talks to me that way.*
"Jean blames me for things I don't do on purpose." *(i.e. not closing the garage door, etc.)*	"Jean shouldn't hold me responsible for something that I cannot remember."	*If I don't remember something, I won't have to deal with the feelings that go with it.*
"Jean has only to ask me and remind me to help with vacation plans."	"I can't take the initiative or the responsibility myself."	*If I take initiative I become responsible; if I take responsibility I could be culpable.*
"I like to be close but I don't always feel like being sexual."	When Jean is physically demonstrative, I become anxious or depressed.	*When we are close, I'm in danger of feeling violated and in danger of having to say no.*
"I thought our sexual relationship was okay, but now I feel she's critical of my lovemaking."	I am being criticized for how I do make love and for how I don't make love. There's no point in doing it at all.	*I don't have an appropriate model for love and sex as the boundaries were corrupted. The best compromise is a non-sexual relationship. To have a better sex life, I'll have to be more in touch with my body, my sexual feelings, and my sexual memories.*

on Jean to be the sexual member of the partnership became more threatening as it impinged on her dissociative defenses. It was not only easier for Marietta to acknowledge the need to work through her sexual abuse history, but it became possible for both Marietta and Jean to discuss each of their sexual needs and fears directly. The dynamic issues of the couple had a way of stimulating each member's individual complementary intrapsychic issues, and vice versa. Both levels had to be addressed sufficiently for the treatment to succeed.

While it might seem that gay or lesbian couples who have been together for several years would come to treatment for help with understandable and identifiable relational conflicts and not be vulnerable to the insidious effects of internalized homophobia, that is not always the case. "Where intrapsychic trauma converges with social stigma, internalized homophobia continues to be an important factor" (Crespi, 2001, p. 78). Furthermore, the importance of addressing a "gay patient's shame and self-hatred" and using the analytic forum to fully understand "the developmental experience" of a patient, has been underscored by Frommer (1994, 1995). A couple is a new family, and after the honeymoon is over, the new family's "internal families" are inevitably activated. Like the culture at large, these internal families contain conscious and unconscious anti-homosexual attitudes — powerful forces that exist and need to be acknowledged. As analysts, we can be aware of these issues as they emerge in the clinical setting, and as couple therapists we need to be even more vigilant in identifying the insidious effect of these internalizations on the dyad.

References

Ackerman, N. (1966), *Treating the Troubled Family*. New York: Basic Books.

Cole, G. (2002), *Infecting the Treatment: Being an HIV-Positive Analyst*. Hillsdale, NJ: The Analytic Press.

Crespi, L. (1995), Some thoughts on the role of mourning in the development of a positive lesbian identity. In: *Disorienting Sexuality: Psychoanalytic Reappraisals of Sexual Identities*, ed.

T. Domenici & R. C. Lesser, New York: Routledge, pp. 19–32.
——— (2001), The bomb in the chrysalis. *J. Gay & Lesbian Psychother.*, 5:77–85.
Drescher, J. (1998), *Psychoanalytic Therapy and the Gay Man.* Hillsdale, NJ: The Analytic Press.
Epstein, L. & Feiner, A. H. (1979), *Countertransference: The Therapist's Contribution to the Therapeutic Situation.* Northvale, NJ: Aronson.
Freud, S. (1914), Remembering, repeating and working through further recommendations in the technique of psychoanalysis: II. *Standard Edition,* 12:147–156. London: Hogarth Press, 1958.
Frommer, M. S. (1994), Homosexuality and psychoanalysis: Technical considerations revisited. *Psychoanal. Dial.,* 4:215–233.
——— (1995), Countertransference obscurity in the psychoanalytic treatment of homosexual patients. In: *Disorienting Sexuality: Psychoanalytic Reappraisals of Sexual Identities,* ed. T. Domenici & R. C. Lesser. New York: Routledge, pp. 65–82.
Glazer, D. (1998), Lesbian mothers: A foot in two worlds. *Psychoanal. & Psychother.,* 16:145–151.
——— (2001), Lesbian motherhood: Restorative choice or developmental imperative? *J. Gay & Lesbian Psychother.,* 4:31–44.
Kohut, H. (1971), *The Analysis of the Self.* New York: International Universities Press.
Margolis, B. (1994), Narcissistic transference: The product of overlapping self and object fields. *Modern Psychoanal.,* 19:139–148.
Ogden, T. (1979), On projective identification. *Internat. J. Psychoanal.,* 61:513–533.
Sandler, J. & Sandler, A. (1978), On the development of object relationships and affects. *Internat. J. Psycho-Anal.,* 59:285–296.
Scharff, D. & Scharff, J. (1991), *Object Relations Couples Therapy.* Northvale, NJ: Aronson.
Spotnitz, H. (1969), *Modern Psychoanalysis of the Schizophrenic Patient.* New York: Human Sciences Press.
Stierlin, H. (1977), *Psychoanalysis and Family Therapy.* New York: Aronson.

6

Teasing Apart Gender, Object Choice, and Motherhood in Lesbian Relationships

Deborah F. Glazer

I n 1942, Helene Deutsch grappled with the issue of a woman's impetus to mother. She saw the wish or motivation to mother as occurring along developmental lines separate from the sexual instincts, object choice, and gender identity. In fact, she spoke of the possibility of the wish to mother existing outside of the realm of sex, gender, and outside of the world of a woman's relationship to men. She saw the wish to mother as a complex developmental outcome, resulting from many developmental pathways, and determined that the striving to mother could be satisfied in a number of nontraditional ways. For example, she discusses woman raising children together.

Another form of motherliness . . . more frequent in America than in other countries . . . may be seen when two women active in some profession, living together in a more or less sublimated friendship, adopt a child. Usually one of the women assumes the role of mother and the other that of family provider. This division of interest is only relative, for usually both women wish to gratify their motherliness. The two complement each other to form a whole of active motherliness in relation to the child [Deutsch, 1945, p. 34].

To Deutsch, these women seemed to live in a foreign country about which she could speculate, but never fully inhabit or understand. Despite her questioning of traditional models of gender and motherhood, Deutsch was not able to address fully many of the important and radical issues she herself had raised. Not until recently have feminist and postmodern analysts (Butler, 1990; Dimen, 1991; Goldner, 1991; O'Connor and Ryan, 1993; Domenici and Lesser, 1995; Glassgold and Iasenza, 1995; D'Ercole, 1996; Magee and Miller, 1997; Schwartz, 1998; Gould and Kiersky, 2001) taken up and expanded on the radical ideas about female sexuality and the impetus to parent found in Deutsch's early work.

In the modern world, gender, sexuality, and motherhood are being reevaluated and are not necessarily viewed as fixed, bio-logically constructed, interdependent truths (Glazer and Drescher, 2001). Psychoanalysis is beginning to move away from a conflation of sexuality and reproduction, a linkage that Deutsch believed allowed for continued sexuality in a culture organized around Judeo-Christian ethics and judgment. Today, mothering is being defined as a function rather than a purpose for sexuality or as a biological imperative. As Schwartz (1998) notes, "The de-construction of gendered motherhood allow[s] us to envisage a new parenting subject that would be less uni-tary and more conditional, a conception of mothering that tran-scends gender" (p. 152).

This postmodern view of mothering as a function can be seen in a children's television show *The Rugrats*. A young boy whose mother has died is being raised by his father. As Mother's Day approaches, he is trying to understand the concept of "mother." His friends describe what a mother is: "She loves you, and feeds you, and takes care of you." In a powerful moment of insight, the child proclaims that he does, in fact, have a mother. It is his father.

Societal definitions of family are changing, in part, due to advances in reproductive technologies, increased availability of adoptions, and advances in gay and lesbian civil rights. Contemporary psychoanalysis is caught in this trend and finds itself moving away from a belief in the causal links between gender, object choice, and maternal strivings. In the process, it remains open how each of these internal identifications and self-representations affect a woman's self-experience and feelings of adequacy. For example, Butler (1995) sees the construction of gender as an outgrowth of a heterosexual paradigm. It is the repudiation of her same-sex desire that allows a woman to feel adequate in her gender. Consequently, "threats to heterosexuality become threats to gender itself. . . . The fear of homosexual desire in a woman may induce a panic that she is losing her femininity; that she is not a woman; that if she is not quite a man, she is like one and hence monstrous in some way" (p. 168).

Like gender beliefs, the wish to mother, and the ability to achieve motherhood, biological or otherwise, can have powerful effects on a woman's self-experience. Notman and Lester (1988) suggest that a woman's "awareness of her reproductive potential is part of her self-esteem" (p. 139). This is the case in cultures where the early experiences and definitions of womanliness are based on a heterosexual or maternal model. According to Dinnerstein (1976), "The deepest root of our acquiescence to the maiming and mutual imprisonment of men and women lies in the monolithic fact of human childhood" (p. 28). Dinnerstein believes the traditional heterosexual model of current family life leads the mother to be the first love object, the first source of gratification, and the first source of punishment. For children, this early connection with the mother shapes their relationship to women and in particular shapes a girl's thoughts about being a woman throughout later life. This implies that a woman's self-perception, gendered expectations, and gender ideals are based on early childhood experiences related to the roles and models of the mother in the traditional, heterosexual family from which she comes. A woman's expectation of how and what she is to be as a woman is often based on her mother's role as wife, mother, and homemaker. So, despite current advances in reproductive technologies and societal freedoms that allow for increased procreative options for lesbian couples, a majority of women have internalized a maternal role that has been more traditionally defined.

While increased reproductive freedoms are allowing more women to make choices about motherhood, some women, both lesbian and heterosexual, are opting to be childless rather than engage in obligatory motherhood. They may have to face internal and external biases insofar as society often views marriage and motherhood as markers of womanhood. Childless lesbians are doubly stigmatized because they cannot rely on traditional signifiers of gender adequacy.

For some women with a powerful wish to mother, the decision to raise a child can have healing effects on early, painful self-representations. This is not to suggest that all women who choose mothering necessarily do so out of an attempt to restore a sense of pride or adequacy in their gender. In the case of the woman who does not express a wish to have a child, analytic exploration can address and reshape the fantasies, ideals, and self-judgments related to gender, gender adequacy, and object choice. In straying from the heterosexual model of their mothers, however, lesbians must navigate through a complex web of sameness and difference, both with the actual mother and with an internalized ideal of mother. For some women, the complex maze of identification and difference, the recognition of same-sex desire, and a belief that her same-sex desire precludes motherhood can result in painful feelings of gender inadequacy. They must come to terms with what it means to be a woman who is not a wife, to be a woman who loves women rather than men, and to be a woman who may not automatically desire to mother.

Clinical Examples
Susan entered analytic treatment complaining of sexual inhibition in her long-term relationship with her lover, Tina. Her sexual inhibition was multiply determined. Susan described herself as a sexually curious child, who enjoyed sexual exploration with both girl and boy playmates. As a child she took pride and pleasure in her body. As puberty approached, however, Susan began to realize that she was more interested in other girls and was increasingly disinterested in sex play with the boys. This left her with powerful feelings of shame and self-doubt.

As an adult, Susan expressed the belief that being a lesbian, and having never experienced intercourse with a man, made her flawed and inadequate. She believed that she was not entitled access into the world of women. This belief was often represented somatically, and Susan was continually self-conscious about her body. She could not tolerate signs of bodily round-ness that she associated with traditional female sexuality. At the same time, she criticized herself for not having the bodily pride and freedom to experience arousal that she felt was the privilege of sexual (meaning heterosexual) women.

Susan also expressed a belief that she could not conceive a child, and that if she did the child would certainly not ade-quately grow within her. She felt this was because she was not a true woman, but rather a "hybrid" who had no rights to wom-anly experiences. Nevertheless she pursued the option of hav-ing a child. Despite her expectations of infertility, Susan conceived on her first alternative insemination and carried a healthy baby to term. For the first time in her adult life, Susan felt proud of her body and experienced herself as belonging to the world of women. Her usual disdain for bodily signs of roundness was overridden by a joy in her growing belly. Her breasts became a source of pride because with them, she could nurse her thriving baby. Susan realized that her same-sex desire did not preclude her womanhood and did not destroy her abil-ity to mother. Although her sexual inhibitions did not fully dis-sipate, Susan began to experience increased desire for emotional and physical intimacy with her lover.

As Crespi (1995) has noted, some women cannot allow them-selves to become mothers in a lesbian relationship because they are unable to mourn sufficiently the heterosexual object and identification. They cannot abandon the wish to conceive a child biologically with their lover. This was the case of Janice, a single, childless lesbian in her early 30s, who expressed this painful state of mind. Because she is a childless lesbian, Janice believes that she is not fully a citizen of the world. She describes herself as living in the dark recesses of society, never fully measuring up to her heterosexual, married friends who have children. She likens herself to Scully, the female federal agent in the television series, *The X-Files*. Janice recounted an episode in which Scully discovered that she had been kidnapped by federal agents and that her eggs had been surgically removed. Janice feels that her lesbianism and her childlessness have left her a damaged as a woman, a mutant created by the laws and lawkeepers of society.

Emma, in contrast to Janice, is more accepting of her lesbian-ism. She is able to allow herself a deep, committed, long-term lesbian relationship. Emma describes a powerful sense of long-ing to be a mother since early childhood. She loves children and volunteers to teach painting to inner city youth. Emma will not allow herself to conceive a child, however, until technology has advanced enough to allow for the melding of two eggs. This wish interferes with her ability to become a mother because this is the only option that she feels she and her lover can pursue in creating a biological child of their own.

This fantasy appeared to have origins in Emma's family mythology. As a child, she was told that she was initially con-ceived as one of two twins but that her sister failed to thrive in utero. Emma's fantasy was that her own greed and competi-tiveness had caused her to eat all the goodies inside her mother, causing her unborn sister to starve. Thus, the reality of carrying a baby while her lover did not felt to Emma like a terribly dan-gerous and destructive competition and a reenactment of her early fantasy of destroying her unborn sibling.

Emma's fantasy is consistent with an earlier observation that as they involve a reengagement of the earliest mother–child bond, experiences of motherhood can sometimes evoke power-ful regressive feelings (Mendell, 1998). In a traditional hetero-sexual family, much of that early relationship requires the small child to deal with maternal power. The mother is seen as the omnipotent source of gratification and punishment. She is like-ly to evoke strong feelings of envy, but her power and the pos-sibility of punishment at her hand makes it too frightening to compete with her (Dinnerstein, 1976; Harris, 1997). Many of these childhood feelings and fears may be reawakened through one's own mothering experience.

For the lesbian couple, these feelings may be particularly intense. Because technology does not currently permit women to conceive together biologically, and because legal co-adoption takes time, a lesbian couple must work out complex issues relat-ed to who carries or adopts the infant. This legal or biological distinction may often result in envy and competition regarding the parental role. As Harris (1997) notes, competition is stereo-typically defined as masculine behavior. Thus, feelings of envy and competition with the lover and coparent can provoke further discomfort in one's experience and sense of gender.

Brenda is a lesbian in her early 40s. She is in a long-term monogamous relationship, and is coparenting a child carried by her lover, Sue. Before this relationship Brenda had been in a heterosexual marriage. During that marriage, she tried for many years to conceive but was finally diagnosed as infertile. Nonetheless, Brenda agreed to raise a child at Sue's request. Brenda and Sue planned and conceived this child together and intended to coparent their child equally. They would both be "mother." Brenda, however, finds it difficult to organize her role as mother. Her relationship with her lover has suffered greatly as a result. Watching Sue conceive, experience pregnancy, and deal with the birth and neonatal period brought up powerful feelings of envy and grief in Brenda. Although she says that she perceives herself to be their son's mother, internally Brenda cannot accept this role.

For Brenda, the experience of comothering evokes feelings of gender inadequacy as well as distressful feelings of envy. She says that she did not feel as comfortable with her son at his birth because she had not known him inside her body as Sue did. In a feeling echoed by many nonbiological lesbian mothers, Brenda felt less equipped to offer him anything soothing and sustaining. Sue had the capacity to soothe their son by nursing him. In keeping with Brenda's past pattern of relationships, she decided to care for him by providing more of the financial and organizational aspects of family life. This left her feeling out of the maternal loop and more identified with her internalized image of father. This exacerbated Brenda's feelings of inauthenticity or lack of authenticity as a mother and heightened her own feelings of grief about her inability to conceive.

A similar dynamic is seen with Jennifer, the mother of a son born to her lover, Tanya. She, too, experienced difficulty with the role of nonbiological lesbian mother. Jennifer felt envy at her lover's relationship with their child. She could not include her lover and son in office functions as she feared that her lover would nurse their child. She believed that seeing Tanya nurse would lead those watching to share Jennifer's view that she was not truly worthy of the term "mother." When Jennifer and her lover wanted a second child, it was decided that Jennifer would carry the child. Whereas previously Jennifer had taken on the role of family provider, Jennifer was now faced with being pregnant, tired, and home much of the time. Although excited by the pregnancy, Jennifer began to envy her lover's freedom to be out in the world.

Some lesbians struggle with feelings of gender inauthenticity, and others find the gender transgression associated with same-sex desire to be gratifying. When the coming-out experience is resolved and feelings of shame and gender inadequacy are worked through, there can be great freedom. In living as a lesbian, a woman can extricate herself from what Dinnerstein (1976) described as imprisonment. She may feel herself capable of moving more fluidly between the stereotypical, socially constructed male and female roles used to define gender, rather than being constrained by the artificial dichotomy these constructs can create. Pregnancy and the early maternal experiences of caring for an infant may intensify the rigid female identifications, while limiting the freedom and power to go out in the world. Physically, the birth mother must face the strenuous process of pregnancy, delivery, and recuperation, while her lover is not physically burdened. The biological mother may envy her lover's freedom to be a mother without having to relinquish the gender freedom her lesbianism allows her.

For both mothers, coparenting a child increases the need to be "out" in the world. A young child may experience no shame at her family constellation, and proudly introduce her two mommies wherever she goes. For women who are reluctant to be known publicly as lesbian, this can be particularly difficult. Cynthia is a biological lesbian mother who is raising a child with her lover, Trudy. They live in a blue-collar, suburban area. Although Cynthia says that she is not conflicted about her lesbianism, she is fearful of the judgments and prejudices of the people in her environment. As her son begins to speak, she is reluctant to teach him to call both of his mothers "Mommy"; she is afraid that his "outing" of his mothers will endanger all of them. For Cynthia, this fear is multiply determined. She has difficulty sharing the role of mother and does

not want to relinquish the part to another woman. She is partly engaged in a competitive battle with her lover for her son's
affections. In addition, Cynthia is living in a conservative
neighborhood at a time when hate crimes are on the rise. Thus,
her fear of assault and discrimination are not just fantasies, but
based on real fears that resonate with intrapsychic ones.

Ironically, lesbian mothers must inevitably recognize that
their children can face the same kind of biases that they, as gay
people, experienced. For many women, antihomoseuxal bias
toward their children can reawaken or exacerbate the painful,
lifelong experiences of being a member of a hated minority.
Brenda and Sue, who were discussed earlier, have a three-year-
old daughter, Annabel, attending preschool. The daughter's
teacher read a storybook about a lesbian family and then asked
all of the children to draw a picture of their families. Annabel
refused to draw her two mothers. In addition, lately she has
been asking more questions about daddies. Brenda and Sue
fear that they have brought a child into the world as part of an
inadequate family — inadequate, that is, in heterosexual
terms. In Butler's (1995) terms, just as they may have mourned
a relinquished heterosexual object for themselves, they will
also have to grieve their inability provide their child a father.

Conclusion

Increasingly, lesbians are enjoying the freedom to become mothers, yet with these new definitions of family, new issues emerge
in the consultation room. Competition between the mothers
related to issues of intimacy, authenticity, and responsibility
may complicate the family dynamic. The child's recognition of
her parents' homosexuality and societal biases expressed
against the child and family may reawaken emotions related to
the mothers' earlier coming out experiences.

Despite such difficulties, however, all the lesbian mothers discussed in this chapter feel that their lives have been greatly
enriched by the maternal experience. They have worked hard to
create and sustain their families. They love their children deeply
and couldn't imagine life without them. Despite the difficulties
they face, they all express deep fulfillment and joy in the maternal
experience.

References

Butler, J. (1990), *Gender Trouble: Feminism and the Subversion of Identity*. New York: Routledge.
——— (1995), Melancholy gender — Refused identification. *Psychoanal. Dial.*, 5:165–180.

Crespi, L. (1995), Some thoughts on the role of mourning in the development of a positive lesbian identity. In: *Disorienting Sexualities*, ed. T. Domenici & R. C. Lesser. New York: Routledge, pp. 19–32.

D'Ercole, A. (1996), Postmodern ideas about gender and sexuality: The lesbian woman redundancy. *Psychoanal. Psychother.*, 13:142–152.

Deutsch, H. (1945), *Psychology of Women, Vol. II*. New York: Grune & Strutton.

Dimen, M. (1991), Deconstructing difference: Gender, splitting, and transitional space. *Psychoanal. Dial.*, 1:335–352.

Dinnerstein, D. (1976), *The Mermaid and the Minotaur: Sexual Arrangements and Human Malaise*. New York: Harper Perennial.

Domenici, T. & Lesser, R. C., eds. (1995), *Disorienting Sexuality: Psychoanalytic Reappraisals of Sexual Identities*. New York: Routledge.

Glassgold, J. & Iasenza, S., eds. (1995), *Lesbians and Psychoanalysis: Revolutions in Theory and Practice*. New York: Free Press.

Glazer, D. F. & Drescher, J., eds. (2001), *Gay and Lesbian Parenting*. New York: Haworth Press.

Goldner, V. (1991), Toward a critical relational theory of gender. *Psychoanal. Dial.*, 1:249–272.

Gould, E. & Kiersky, S., eds. (2001), *Sexualities Lost and Found: Lesbians, Psychoanalysis and Culture*. Madison, CT: International Universities Press.

Harris, A. (1997), Aggression, envy and ambition: Circulating tensions in women's psychic life. *Gender & Psychoanal.*, 2:291–325.

Magee, M. & Miller, D. (1997), *Lesbian Lives: Psychoanalytic Narratives Old and New*. Hillsdale, NJ: The Analytic Press.

Mendell, D. (1998), An exploration of three typical maternal fantasies: The cornucopia fantasy, the fantasy of parthenogenesis, and the one-body fantasy. *Psychoanal. Psychother.*, 16:85–110.

Notman, M. T. & Lester, E. (1988), Pregnancy: Theoretical considerations. *Psychoanal. Inq.*, 8:139–169.

O'Connor, N. & Ryan, J. (1993), *Wild Desires and Mistaken Identities: Lesbianism & Psychoanalysis*. New York: Columbia University Press.

Schwartz, A. E. (1998), *Sexual Subjects: Lesbians, Gender, and Psychoanalysis*. New York: Routledge.

7

The Lesbian "Great American Sperm Hunt"

*A Sociological Analysis of Selecting Donors
and Constructing Relatedness*

Laura Mamo

I n 1996, a story appeared in *Harper's Bazaar* magazine claiming that in the Park Slope neighborhood of Brooklyn, "the lesbian paradigm had shifted from playing softball in the park to pushing strollers down the avenue" (Jetter, 1996, p. 66). The article made an intriguing claim that although having babies was not a new feature of the lesbian community, the popularity of so-called turkey baster babies had gained momentum throughout the 1980s. By the turn to the 21st century, several sperm banks were targeting their services specifically to lesbians and finding it difficult to meet the demand for their services. In 2002, a for-profit online sperm bank, ManNotIncluded.com, opened to provide lesbian couples with sperm for home insemination. In one day, 3000 lesbian couples had signed up to receive services, and 5000 men had registered to be sperm donors. The founder said, "We have been overwhelmed by the response to the Web site. Over 40,000 people have visited the Web site since it went live. . . . As a result of this interest we've demonstrated that there is a huge demand for our unique service" (Associated Press, 2002).

Lesbians, it seemed, were increasingly turning to biomedical organizations such as semen banks to meet their pregnancy goals. Although the turkey baster baby was alive and well theoretically, in practice, something more *biomedical* was underway. To better understand the meanings and practices of lesbians getting pregnant, including the experiences of donor selection, 34 lesbians in the process of trying to conceive and 6 sperm bank providers and fertility experts providing services to lesbians were interviewed. In this chapter, I present an analysis of donor selection processes. A central idea that emerges throughout women's experiences with semen selection is how profoundly these experiences are shaped by biomedical and medical marketing processes (see Clarke et al., 2003, for a sociological analysis of biomedicalization). For lesbians, the social experience of "being" a lesbian and wanting to conceive is transformed into a biomedical experience through their biomedical classification as "infertile" and its consequences for shaping their reproductive experiences (see Mamo, 2002, for a complete analysis of lesbian reproduction).

In analyzing lesbian processes of selecting semen donors, this study found that lesbians engage in processes of constructing relatedness and explicates what might be called affinity ties. Affinity ties illustrate the ways in which women negotiate cultural discourses of "appropriate" family forms as they construct notions of relatedness. This research found that women's experiences with achieving pregnancy include deliberate constructions of relatedness through the selection of both the "source" of semen and the selected donor traits.

The "Great American Sperm Hunt"

In analyzing where and how women obtain sperm, the ways in which they describe their decision concerning which type of donor to choose were examined. Women largely selected between two donor types: (1) initially unknown donors drawn from sperm banks and (2) known donors, often termed directed donors, drawn from women's personal social networks.

An unknown donor is selected from a sperm bank and, if anonymous, the identity of the donor will never be known to the woman or to the child. A variation on this is an identity-release donor, who is also selected from a sperm bank but, in contrast, the identity of the donor is made available to the child, if he or she chooses, after the child reaches 18 years of age.

These donors are also often termed "yes donors" and are in high demand among lesbian consumers of sperm bank services (as discussed in the next section). In contrast, a known or directed donor allows a range of potential constructions of relatedness to the parent(s) and child(ren): from acknowledgment as the donor to full coparent status. This choice to use a known donor is influenced by a host of factors that often require negotiation. For example, thinking through the degree to which a known donor will or will not participate in a potential child's and mother's or mothers' lives is commonplace: will his identity be the only part he plays beyond conception (i.e., someone who the parent(s) can describe to the child), will he become an "uncle" figure, or will he perform as both a biological and social father and coparent the potential child(ren)? Frequently, choosing what type of donor to use involves conceptualizing "health": Is the donor perceived to be in "good" physical and mental health? What does "good health" mean? When potential mothers choose to use a known donor, they may ask that his semen undergo the same "screening" and testing services required at sperm banks or may ask a series of screening questions to ascertain his health status. In known-donor arrangements, the relatedness of a donor to the potential parent(s) and child(ren) is negotiated outside of sperm banks and can take many forms.

Women's decisions regarding what type of donor to use were shaped by multiple factors including cultural influences, legal issues, desires for social legitimacy, and women's complex feelings regarding biology and social connection. At times, these decisions also included thinking through perceived and real feelings of multiple other actors — one's partner (if she has one), one's friends and family members, the known donor and his relatives, the unknown donor, and even the imagined potential child. Thus, making decisions regarding what type of donor to use and what characteristics to choose are highly social processes. Other factors include age, physical health, cost, and insurance status. Examples include the selection of known donors when women are financially unable to purchase semen or when women choose not to access biomedical services; the selection of anonymous donors when women are over 35 years old or diagnosed with a "in/fertility" issue allowing them access to technologically advanced treatment protocols that often rule out the use of fresh sperm from a known donor; and the selection of anonymous donors when one perceives emotional and legal risks associated with using a known donor. The most frequent reason women gave for accessing a semen donor through a sperm bank was the desire to minimize legal and emotional entanglements by securing both biological and legal ties with children.

In general, processes of finding sperm include negotiating the type of relatedness desired for one's potential family; choosing an active father, an inactive father, or no father; using currently known friends or relatives or finding new acquaintances for sperm donation; or choosing to go through sperm banks. It spans the emotional spectrum from negotiating legal contracts and formal agreements to the intimate and often emotionally wrought process of asking friends to find or be sperm donors. Like other moments along the process, the quest for sperm can alternately involve explicit intentionality, fluidity, and a necessity for many revisions and complex negotiations.

The Power of Knowing: Choosing a Known Donor
In negotiating possible parameters of social connection among the donor, parent(s), and offspring, women ask themselves multiple questions concerning parental "rights," social relationships, and legal implications. The majority of women interviewed had at one point considered seeking semen from someone they know. One participant, Chloe, described where she and her partner are in the achieving pregnancy process. She replied with this statement: "Oh sure, we are right at the point of the great American sperm hunt. We are very actively looking for a donor, going through our lists of friends and friends of friends and their friends, and trying to go to groups and trying to increase our contacts with other men." For women who choose known donors, but do not yet have someone to fill this role, the hunt for sperm infuses everyday life. This is nowhere more evident than when I asked Arlene, Chloe's partner, to describe the process of finding a donor. She paused, stared at me, and asked, "Well, do you have any friends?"

In these narratives, the meaning of these initial actions to select a donor from one's personal connections appeared to be shaped by a dominant U.S. cultural narrative of identity as knowing one's origins or roots and by a cultural narrative of kin connection as rooted in biological ties. When women choose to engage a known donor, three possibilities exist: (1) relatives of the nonbiological mother, (2) long-term friends, and (3) new acquaintances. Although some women discussed relatives of the "nonbio mom" as a possible solution to the decision of type of donor to use, no one had secured this type of donor arrangement. Kaye describes her and her partner's process:

> [My partner's] brother's name is Ray. At first I thought it would be very nice if Ray was willing to help us out because I felt that [my partner's] family would feel more like the child was actually part of their family. But when he said, "No," he didn't say flat out "No." He said, "I have some issues around this. I think I'd rather not. If it's really, really important to you, let's talk about it some more." Alison decided that she didn't want to pursue it with him. I really think if we were going to use someone who wasn't anonymous, that was the strongest contender because at least there was a reason to confront all those issues.

Upon further discussion, the importance of biological connection emerges as central to this narrative. If this pathway is pursued, both women could be biologically related to the child (i.e., by blood and genetics). But even more important is the perception that this relationship would create "better," "tighter," or more close-knit connections for all family members.

For some women, having a known donor is not only preferable but an essential element in their family formation. These women want the donor to be known to and a part of the child's life, albeit with different degrees of involvement. This was not an element that these women would revise, although the type of agreement and extent of relationship with the donor was more flexible. For example, when Carla began pursuing insemination, she wanted to form a coparenting agreement with a close male friend. Early in our interview she talked about a close friend

whom she had met in a therapy group. They had decided to
coparent together and after two years of trying, he changed his
mind. Despite this interruption, Carla remains committed to the
idea of her child knowing the father.

> Well, that's been more of the struggle part for me. It's inter-
> esting, because I really wanted to have that. . . . I feel like I am
> going to cry. [Cries for a minute or more.] I really wanted to
> have, I really wanted to have a situation where I knew the
> father and the child knew the father, because of my own back-
> ground where I didn't know my father.

Carla's commitment stems from her own biography and the
absence of her own father in her life. For her, the more flexible
elements included the father being a gay man whom she knew
and someone who would be interested in coparenting. As time
progressed and she developed a committed relationship with a
female partner, these flexible criteria were constantly renegoti-
ated and reconfigured. Despite her acknowledgment that "there
are a lot of options," the essential criterion of having the donor
known to the child remained stable. Although it was originally
an ideal to know and have a history with the father, she revised
her plan to include a known donor who the child will know as
his or her father: "I'm being more open . . . There are still things
I am attached to . . . I am attached to the child knowing who the
biological father is even if he is not in the child's life that much."
    Chloe and Arlene also want to use a known donor. In contrast
to Carla, these women want a donor and not a parent. Arlene
describes her and her partner's process as follows:

> We have talked about anonymous and known donors, and we
> have also considered having a coparent of some fashion,
> either an uncle or an occasional person who would spend
> some time with the child. But [we decided] anonymous
> would be easier [for us] legally and difficult for the child.
> Knowing that children want to *know* things. Also having had
> a lover that was adopted and didn't know her parents, which
> drove her nuts. While adoption doesn't do that for everyone,
> I wanted the child to be able to say "okay fine, who was the

donor?" So those are the things that are important to me. How is it going to impact the child? There are things that are criteria for the people we ask. They have to know they want to be donors and not coparents. Most of the men we meet at Prospective Queer Parents (PQP) want to be coparents. If they don't want to be a known donor, that is a problem. People change over time, and I worry about those changes over time. So I think it is really, really important for us that the donor know they want to be a known donor and what that means. For us it means at some point in time when the child asks, "Who is my daddy?" we can say that you have two mommies but your donor is so and so and then they can choose what they want to do about that. The child may want to make a parent out of that person, depending on the culture, and there is no way to know what the child is going to want to do. Children tend to have personalities all on their own.

Finally, a third type of known donor discussed frequently by these respondents is new acquaintances. In this case, the process of finding a suitable donor usually starts with making lists of everyone you know, male and female, to begin getting the word out. Before the emergence of the now well-developed sperm bank industry and greater social acceptability of queer reproduction, lesbians often turned to their gay male friends as sperm donors or enlisted heterosexual friends to serve as "go-betweens." The heterosexual woman would ask a man to be the donor, and only she would know the identities of the donor and recipient. The go-between had the role of arranging for a donor who would relinquish any parental rights, and she would transport the semen from the donor to the "recipient" to ensure confidentiality. In this case, the go-between is also responsible for maintaining the anonymity of all parties. At times, two "go-betweens" have been used to lend an increased sense of legal and emotional security to the intended confidentiality of the transaction (Kendell, 1996). In less formal arrangements, friends are asked to simply find a male from their social networks who would be willing to provide his semen and to discuss with the mother(s)-to-be his future role in the child's life.

By the early 1980s, the AIDS epidemic not only began to take its toll on gay men, but also created fears and alarm over "contagion." This both complicated donor-type choices and led to the high rate of sperm bank use among lesbians. In addition to the legal dangers of the "go-between" method, certain health risks are associated with using an unknown donor whose sperm is not screened for HIV and other sexually transmitted diseases. Even if the donor reports to the "go-between" that he has been screened for health problems, without testing, there is no guarantee that the unknown donor's sperm is actually disease-free and safe to use. Thus, many women use "directed donors" with a "go-between" who arranges with the donor to deposit his semen in a sperm bank for quarantine and testing, before insemination.

By the mid-1990s, as AIDS represented more of a controlled infectious disease, gay and lesbian communities returned to their community roots. As Saffron (1994, p. 99) argues, "My impression is that there is a trend toward more women choosing to know the donor's identity rather than having anonymous donors." Deborah described her process as closely linked with the AIDS epidemic. In California for graduate school, she returned to the midwest to visit a close gay male friend who was dying of AIDS. At this visit, she became close with one of her friend's caregivers. After her friend died, Deborah returned for his funeral. She and the man began talking about their sadness, loss, and their desire to add life to the world. She told him she wants to be a mother and that she had hoped their mutual friend could have lived to be a father to her child. The friend asks if he could do this with her. She is thrilled, but knows she cannot coparent with him, and she wants to be the sole parent. As she described, "Unfortunately, when it came time to write the contract, he backed out. Mostly because I was firm that I wanted to be the sole parent." Disappointed, Deborah returned to California. She described the events that unfolded upon her return:

> I had some neighbors who were watching my cats. And I came back disappointed and told them what had happened. A couple of days later they came back over. They are a heterosexual unmarried couple. And the guy said: "Well, if you would have me, I would be willing to be the donor if you

really want to do this." I was surprised! I was really happy because he is a really sweet guy and he is the donor and he has been through a lot to be the donor. I said let me think about it and let me ask a lot of really very personal questions that I really had no business asking.

In addition to using personal networks, placing advertisements in gay newspapers and on gay Web sites, and attending gay-specific networking and support groups are common resources for women and men who want to parent to meet. This points to an alternative "queer" organizational network for reproductive options. Arlene also described Prospective Queer Parents as providing her with the opportunity to "practice" asking men if they would become a sperm donor: " The support group is good for checking men out, and it has been good for the actual talking to men and getting some practice."

Whether choosing a known donor who is a relative, a friend, or a new acquaintance, negotiations with these men concerning the type of relationship are necessary. Those women who choose and locate specific known donors to be either coparents or donors describe often-elaborate processes of negotiation with these men. For example, Deborah described an initial conversation she had with a man who agreed to be a donor:

You know, he is a totally open guy and really sweet. He assured me he was monogamous and had had a negative AIDS test in the last year but he hadn't had one since. He had a history with alcohol and drug use problems. I asked him when was the last time he used and he said it had been a couple of years, five years. Although it was a serious topic, the prospective donor and his partner had become my best friends, so we were able to have a fairly laid back conversation about him becoming a sperm donor.

We were both a little uncomfortable because these are really personal questions. But it turned out the things I was concerned about were okay . . . And I told him that I wanted to be the sole parent and I wasn't going to ask for anything except for his sperm and, "I don't want you to consider yourself a parent. I am never going to call you a father." He agreed to this and understood that I wanted contact and for the child to be able to make contact with him at any time. So we agreed he would be a known donor with no rights or responsibilities. And he said, "Good because if you wanted a parent I never would do it." So that is how that worked. So he is the donor.

Far from being a predominantly legal and logistical arrangement, however the process of choosing a donor is one that often involves a close coupling of emotions, donation issues, and the importance of the gay community. Carla described the process of reaching such an agreement as a four-year pursuit:

So for the past four years, I have been working with the same person trying to figure this out. He's a friend of mine. I brought it up in an (informal) therapy group. I said that I had decided to do this and I was really going to start pursuing it. I had just been out of a relationship for a few years with a woman and I decided I really want to do this and that I really needed to start moving on it even though I am not in a relationship. [Pause. She starts to cry.] Because I thought I would, I would be in a relationship and then I would be able to decide to do it [crying gets stronger] I'm sorry . . . [pause]. I wanted it to be [crying continues] I wanted it to be a gay man that I knew. And the person I had talked to a long time ago in the beginning has AIDS so that became impossible.

In Carla's narrative, the link between community and family formation within the gay community is raised in her desire for the donor to be a gay man.

Once agreements are reached, more formal written contracts become important. It is interesting that in all the cases in which women negotiated known-donor contracts, the women located sample contracts from either queer books or local resources and not from biomedical resources. They then modified these to fit their own needs. Kim described this as follows:

For a long time, we had an informal agreement. Then I drew up a contract from the National Center for Lesbian Rights. I just copied it pretty much verbatim and changed a few things.

When I gave it to Bruce he signed it, and I signed it, too. So, we have that. It pretty much states that he has no rights or responsibilities for the child. So I can't ask him for money and he can't take the kid. It's not legal, not binding in the state of California.

In sum, processes of achieving pregnancy are fraught with complex negotiations and strategies to manage divergent issues such as legal and emotional considerations; relationships with family members, friends, and communities; one's own personal biography; access to resources; and cultural and subjective meanings of family and relatedness.

Choosing an Unknown Donor: Negotiating Legal and Emotional Entanglements

While legal, social, and emotional entanglements shape many women's decisions to select a known donor, the decision to choose an unknown donor requires formulating constructing social connections with semen and imagined donors. In California, the Family Code Section 7613(b) states that "the donor of semen provided to a licensed physician and surgeon for use in artificial insemination of a woman other than the donor's wife is treated in law as if he were not the natural father of a child thereby conceived." The law is designed to protect married heterosexuals who use donor insemination as a result of male infertility. In this case, the woman's husband is legally regarded as the father. Thus, embedded in the law are parameters for who has legal jurisdiction over insemination (a licensed physician and surgeon). Also implicit in that law is the assumption that women who are recipients of donor semen are legally married. If a known donor's semen is used without the transfer of his semen to a sperm bank or licensed physician, then the donor can be granted legal parental rights. If, however, a donor gives his semen to a physician who then hands it to the woman to be inseminated, even if she inseminates herself, the donor is not the legal father. Therefore, unless lesbians choose to inseminate via sperm banks or through a licensed physician, the California Family Code legislates parental rights based on biological ties and, thus, does not secure lesbian parental rights over and against those of a donor. Thus, in practice, clinics and professionals stand in for "paternity." Institutionalized hetero-sexism is embedded in both jurisprudence and biomedicine.

The lesbians interviewed for this study are quite familiar with these laws, and their decisions to use sperm banks reflect this knowledge. Combined with legal considerations are emotional issues.

Rachel expresses her concern about future emotional problems that could arise after a donor sees and gets to know the child:

> I had some male friends who offered and that's when [my partner] and I both decided that it would be better to be anonymous because there are too many emotional issues that could become a problem. I think that you can never under estimate a biological bond even if the individual says they have no interests. I think once they see the child, it is a differ-ent story and that um, pretty much propelled me to go the anonymous route.

Shaping these concerns and decisions are a host of contem-porary social, legal, and cultural forces regulating lesbian and gay legal rights. Due to a long history of court cases involving child custody, women are considering not only real actors in their decision making, but also imagined actors. These imagined actors are the anonymous donors as well as family members of donors who, by law, often have more legal rights over the off-spring than a mother who does nor have a biological connection to the child. An example is a court case in which a deceased donor's parents sued for custody of a child born through known-donor insemination. It is believed that the donor's par-ents were declared the legal grandparents based on their bio-genetic ties to the offspring and were subsequently granted custody. Carmen and Angela were aware of such legal cases and, as they describe, this influenced their decisions.

> We did not want there to be any chance that somebody would come along [with a] paternity suit and want to share parent-ing. We wanted to do all the parenting ourselves. We never even explored using [a known donor] . . . I didn't want to ask anybody and we didn't want to have to deal with it.

Another woman, Esther, had previously pursued meeting gay men interested in coparenting, but then revised her plans, in large part because of the long history of custody cases involving lesbian mothers, cases that most often end with the lesbian mother losing custody. She describes her fear of emotional entanglements:

> I don't want anyone else to have any legal rights over my child. I think that's just 'cause I've seen horrible custody stuff. I just had real fears. You hear the horror stories of the donor who comes back. Or the donor who died and his parents sued for custody based on the best interests for the child *not* being with gay parents. I was not taking any risks. I don't want anybody, I used to say that all the time, "I don't want anyone else to have any legal rights over my child."

Thus, women commonly revised their plans repeatedly as new information, resources, and factors emerge. Each relationship seemed complex in its own right and became even more so through constant engagement in a flow of negotiations that often included multiple others.

Frequently, the first consideration that prompted women to pursue an unknown-donor route is their feelings regarding the involvement of a donor in future parenting. This includes the meaning and place of "fathers" in the potential child's life. Constructing the name and parameters of social connection (i.e., extent of the relationship) a donor will or will not have to a child is an early and highly consequential step in constructing social and familial ties. For Chloe, an essential criterion she holds is "a donor and not a parent." Speaking of a man her sister introduced to her, she says, "I don't think he meets my basic criteria, which is of a level of maturity where they know the difference between donation and parenting." Shari says, "We wanted to keep it as simple as possible, and we wanted to be the primary parents, without any complications." A desire to avoid complications and to keep things "simple" is a common position among women interviewed. Judith described this position well:

> We wanted to keep it as simple as possible. For us, in the way we choose our family, we feel that there is enough difficulty

in getting consensus between two people, let alone four people. So we didn't want a nice couple of gentlemen being coparents with us. We wanted to keep our family simple, with
just the two of us being moms.

Choosing unknown donors represents a means to both minimize legal risks and to avoid the complications and complexities
involved with finding and negotiating with a known donor. Yet
questions concerning biological ancestry, health history, psychological profile, and the meaning of one's identities saturated the
women's decision processes. This aspect of achieving pregnancy
is complex, entangled, and negotiated. Lesbians enact intentional, albeit complicated and constantly revisioned, decisions
regarding the type of semen donor to use. Selecting the type of
donor represents one aspect of achieving pregnancy where plans
must be, and frequently are, revised. Revising plans, then, points
to the contingent nature of the process, subject to constant reconsideration, jettisoning old plans and creating new ones based on
one's current social networks, other people's feelings and
involvement, and how the "great American sperm hunt" is pro-
gressing.

**"As Long as We Have the Choice": Constructing Relatedness
Through Interactions with Sperm Banks**
Two thirds of the women in this sample used sperm bank services. Yet even in this seemingly anonymous setting, this research
found that lesbians interact with the available materials and
information in attempts to construct what can be called affinity
ties. The word "affinity" signals relationship defined by likeness, not by blood. It is used to describe how lesbians imagine
potential social relationships formed through assisted conception using donor semen. To analyze these experiences, interviews and observation with several local sperm banks were
conducted to explore their strategies for marketing and deliver-
ing sperm bank services.

Affinity ties emerged in women's experiences as they translated donor catalog listings into potential relationships.
Through their interactions with donor catalogs, lesbians envision social connections with potential children as formed by

shared social, cultural, and ancestral histories. Within the context of sperm bank organizations, women are presented with
donor catalogs and asked to select the donor (and his given
traits), thus to select the contributing biogenetic material for
their potential child(ren). Women's narratives of their selection
criteria emphasize personality traits and other social characteristics as significant determinants of who or what semen they
would select. Because these characteristics are provided,
because they can choose, women do so. Their choices are thus
embedded in the practice and structures of the organizations in
which they are situated. Furthermore, these biomedical organizations profoundly shape the meanings and experiences of
achieving pregnancy for lesbians.

The commodification and the construction of consumer mar-
kets emerge as central to lesbian experiences with donor selection. Consumerism dictates that there is no choice but to always
exercise choice. Because one can buy semen, the next question is
what type of semen is purchased. Sperm banks have followed
business principles by marketing semen in ways that list difference and thus construct "choices." Today, a common marketing
strategy of semen banks is to provide online and print "short"
donor catalogs to prospective consumers (for a complete analysis of these listings, see Schmidt and Moore, 1998). In these short
catalogs, differences are represented through characteristics
such as race and ethnicity, height, weight, eyes, hair, body-build,
complexion, hobbies, and personality characteristics. Placing
these attributes along a grid structure allows recipients to com-
pare across donors and select "the right semen for the job"
(Clarke and Fujimura, 1992).

As one respondent, June, said, "I'm sure you know or have
heard stories about how odd it is to kind of go shopping for a
donor in those catalogs and online." Similarly, Renee said, "It's
kind of like buying a husband." The commodification of semen
was frequently discussed with unease among the respondents
in this research. Esther said, "It feels really weird to just walk in
off the street and pick up, you know, a bottle of sperm off the
shelf and pay for it. So, we decided to go the known-donor
route." Esther articulates how she and her partner consciously
and intentionally decided not to use a sperm bank explicitly

because of the commodification of semen. She also said, "I feel like lesbians trying to get pregnant is a whole market. Prices continue to rise . . . I really feel like, 'Oh! Here's a market that doesn't have a lot of options, so, we [can] increase prices and they'll still come.'" These women recognize that lesbians have emerged as a consumer market for sperm banks and that the industry has responded with the creation of what the *New York Times* health reporter Gina Kolata has labeled "Fertility Inc." (Kolata, 2002).

After reviewing short forms and selecting three "top picks," lesbians pay for long profiles (available for a fee of $15 – $25) on these donors. In analyzing these stories, this research found that lesbians do read the catalogs in ways that rematerialize the donors into human form. That is, as personality characteristics are marketed and include open-ended descriptions of hobbies, interests, reasons for becoming a sperm donor, life goals, and so on, women selecting semen put these personality characteristics into discourse and translate these descriptions into inheritable characteristics.

Women frequently discussed donor attributes such as clarity of handwriting, articulateness, perceived empathy and generosity, and so on.

Through the short and long forms, sperm banks are communicating to consumers that when they are selecting donor semen, they are selecting potential social, cultural, and biological characteristics to materialize in their offspring, placing their decisions within familiar discourses of genetics and the valuation of particular social attributes. By presenting social characteristics of the donors in donor catalog listings, sperm banks inscribe semen with social and cultural differences and imply that these acquired characteristics may be inheritable ones. This profoundly shapes lesbian experiences with semen marketing materials.

Selecting Donors, Constructing Affinities
Lesbians reconstruct biological characteristics in ways that allow for ambiguities and uncertainties present in beliefs about nature and nurture and allow for the possibility that their choices between different donors are meaningful ones. One way in

which this occurs is through the rematerialization of semen into imagined social actors. As Janella describes, "once we reviews the catalogs, we gave the guys names and stuff. We would be driving and say, 'Oh there's Juan!' based on the nationality and other attributes provided by the sperm bank listings. Once we gave them a name, they were like novel characters. They became these people, and we would get attached to who they are, what they look like." Relatedness, then, incorporates cultural and physical traits. Affinity ties represent this relationality: potential mothers select donor characteristics they might share with the potential offspring. These are not only physical attributes, but also social and cultural ones. In this way, both biogenetic and social ties mark relatedness. Thus, known biogenetic ties are replaced by what I call affinity ties in constructing relatedness.

Affinity ties are made possible through the elaboration of semen as possessing (1) personality, hobbies, and other social characteristics; (2) knowing where one comes from; (3) health and a health history; and (4) as possessing an ethnic identity. In many ways, the "new genetics" has created a proliferation of beliefs in genetic inheritance, marked by an explosion of research in genetics and genetic inheritance. So much so that in the words of one woman, "My family and I were calling it genetic engineering." These activities are consequential for notions of relatedness. Donor selection is a site in which people experience, interact with, and come to understand ideologies of genetic inheritance, particularly within contexts of family and kin relations. In addition, subjects actively construct a new cultural discourse of affinity ties as concomitant with biogenetic relatedness.

First, one of the more important qualities that women in the Bay Area consider when choosing either a known or unknown donor is one who comes from a desired "racial and ethnic background." Race and ethnicity were discussed as both a form of "matching" (i.e., a desire for a child who resembles the nonbiological mom) and as a form of sharing cultural and ancestral roots. In analyzing how women understand and construct these elements as important, users select sperm based on a notion of relatedness that emphasizes ambiguities among knowing one's biological identities and sharing social subjectivities. That is, they maintain a liminal space between biogenetic and social ties. Women who select known donors outside of the sperm bank infrastructure (either as coparents or in some other capacity) emphasize cultural ideals of relatedness and social connection in much the same way as women who select "yes" donors from sperm banks. For those women who chose to locate sperm through sperm banks, their actions highlight the ways in which assisted reproduction is not only a technical process, but also a social and cultural one.

Constructions of race and ethnicity in women's narratives were mediated through discourses of relatedness in such a way that they were taken for granted. This occurs through the close coupling of race and ethnicity with origin; origin stories operate as mechanisms of social relatedness by emphasizing matching, identity, and knowing. These stories were told through the discourse of "identity" or likeness to one's family or the family of the nonbirth mom. Matching or the desire for potential offspring to resemble either the biological mom or the nonbiological mom in terms of race and ethnicity was central to the women's choices. This desire to match is not a straightforward "let's make a baby that looks like me" process. Although some sperm banks provide photo-matching services, for a fee, in which they look at a picture of the donor and match it to a picture of the biological or nonbiological mom, none of the women interviewed used this service (but sperm banks have only recently started offering it). For these women, affinity includes shared racial and ethnic background and shared social and physical characteristics. Depending on the sperm bank, ethnic characteristics are listed in terms of national ancestry (e.g., Dutch, German, and Italian) or as racial phenotype (e.g., Caucasian, Hispanic). As stated earlier, I argue that the power of knowing ones "roots" or genetic lineage is central to donor selection processes. Nonetheless, although women often select donors by "matching" racial and ethnic characteristics of the donor to those of mother(s)-to-be, this "match" emphasizes race as social and cultural ancestry not as a biogenetic characteristic. Thus, in my formulation of affinity ties, affinity emphasizes "knowing" one's ancestral past as much as it emphasizes resembling one's social family in appearance.

In an interview with Shari and Robin, the nonbiological mother identified as Latina. In this case, a key criterion for donor selection includes Spanish and Mexican ancestry based on the partner's biography. "He's three quarters Spanish and a quarter Mexican with green eyes, and that fits her most, you know. The dark hair and everything." In this case, ethnic origin stands in for physical looks. This respondent continues to discuss the idea of having "mixed children":

> Having mixed children is social, too. I think that in this environment and this society, it's better not to be identified one way or the other. My ideal world is where everybody's a little blend of something, you know. I think that's a better way. And I think that is how people are learning to get along on a social basis. They are not identified as this or I'm that, but just, they're a person . . . I selected someone with a Latino mix for that reason. And dark, dark features. He's like 5'11", 170 pounds. Nice, trim, athletic guy, you know, that kind of stuff. He's educated. Has a big family and no health problems. They did all that screening for us.

Affinity ties provide legitimacy in everyday interactions with heteronormative society. Looking like and being like someone accomplishes "true" familyhood. June described this well:

> Did the donor look enough like both of us that the child would look enough like both of us? That it wouldn't be a constant um, kind of, flag in the world that this wasn't *really* our child? And I know that a lot of other people who deal with that, certainly with international adoptions and interracial adoptions, and it's not insurmountable. But we were, since we had enough similar coloring, the two of us, we thought to have a donor who also had similar coloring.

Again, race and ethnicity emerges as central to the construction of social and familial legitimacy. If the child looks enough like the parents that he or she will feel comfortable and so that in everyday interactions with others, people will not question the family's legitimacy.

Racial and ethnic characteristics were used as a means by which to "match" against oneself or one's partner's background. This matching, in my analysis, signals a strategy by which to maximize affinity. Racial origin stories are constructed as a means by which women come to "know" a donor's racial/ethnic identity, and thereby, the identity of a yet to be born child. Yet women often begin processes using such methodic and self-conscious criteria, but quickly these change. Marilyn explains this well:

> I started off trying to match the men in my family, blonde, blue eyed, 6 feet, 180, Irish, English sort of, Northern European extraction. And then I got side tracked, and I was like, oh, he sounds cute, oh, he sounds really cute. And then I ended up choosing a donor who was Black-Irish with black hair, blue eyes, very fair skin. I thought, he sounds really cute . . . So it became this nonintellectual decision. I started off very intellectual and became very nonintellectual. So that was kind of fun.

In the beginning, these women incorporated phenotype into their selection criteria as a means of mixing or blending together. This, of course, is not an unusual cultural discourse for reproduction and is one heterosexuals "naturally" use. But what makes this interesting is the revision. The respondent describes the shift away from the "romanticism" of "putting her into me" to a functional selection criteria based on sperm count. As the process of achieving pregnancy continued, she, like many, became less concerned with maximizing and mimicking the appearance of biogenetic ties through racial matching. They shift away from incorporating phenotype into their selection criteria as a means of mixing or blending together and achieving seeming racial affinity. Over time, they experienced the impracticality of imagining such blending and opted for more functional criteria.

This revision is the reverse of what I usually found, where things began methodically and became "irrational" and "out of control."

Second, I found identity release or "yes donors" to be an important selection criterion for women because of the significance of the possibility for their children to "know where they came from." Women asked themselves, What would it mean to get a phone call? What would it mean for the child, for the parent(s)? For potential siblings or others in one's social circle? One woman described choosing a yes donor as follows:

> Probably the biggest criterion was having a "yes donor." 'Cause we just thought as parents that would seem like kind of a nice thing to do to at least leave that open to the kids just to have the option to find out who the donor was, where he or she came from.

Another couple also placed primary importance on "yes donors." In this scenario, Michelle did not, at first, feel strongly about the importance of "knowing" one's origin. She attributes this insistence on knowing to American cultural ideals. As an Italian, she described never questioning one's identity and social belonging. Once in the United States she experienced two issues that she described as shaping her decisions. One was the importance of identity. "Identity politics is so prevalent here. Everyone defines themselves based on their culture and ancestry," she said, "I was not used to that." She then described a friend who was adopted and had a difficult time "not knowing where she came from." In the following quote, Paula also describes the importance of a willing-to-be-known donor on her decision. Here, however, this attribute led her to consider personality attributes as well, not because they might be genetically inheritable, but because they provide a window into the donor's response when the 18-year-old child makes that phone call: "We basically said the only option for us was the one where at least our child would get one phone call [to the sperm donor]. At least have that closure. That was real important to us."

It is interesting that the "one phone call" is understood here as closure, and not an opening-up of possibilities. This, I argue, highlights the importance of social and cultural ancestry, of knowing one's roots, as significant to creating "identity" and a form of wholeness in U.S. culture. The phone call to the donor symbolizes a means to know oneself and to close the unanswered question of who I am and where I come from. Knowing and asserting one's identity as origin is a dominant U.S. cultural narrative.

Third, health and health history of the donor and his immediate family are said to be significant characteristics considered in their selection processes. Here, women engaged in a process of understanding their own health and family health history in relation to the donor's. Their decision became a way of reducing risk for the potential child. For example, if breast cancer was present in a biological mom's family, a donor with no cancer in his family would be chosen. As one respondent said, "We looked at alcohol and cancer and decided to rule out anybody with these histories. We don't really know, but we decided we should rule them out to be safe." This desire to "be safe" symbolizes an active attempt to reduce health risks for the potential child. Another respondent discussed the importance she placed on all health factors, but most important were a history of allergies and high blood pressure. It is an idea that many women in this research emphasized. It is also important to note that some donors were also selected not to reduce risk, but to enhance familial qualities (e.g., choosing a tall donor if one is short). As Joyce said,

My family and I were calling it genetic engineering [laughter] . . . I picked ones that I thought were possibilities for me . . . I ruled out ones that were nationalities different from me then I chose donors that were similar to me, that shared my interests. Next, I thought, 'what are the things I wouldn't want the donor to have?' and I ruled out cancer history, acne, any signs of poor health.

These are significant in that she emphasizes characteristics she deems to be inheritable. The dominant discourse of the gene and genetic inheritance emerges here. Today, with the Human Genome Project and heightened scrutiny of genes as causal factors in one's health, donor selection processes draw deeply on this discourse.

Finally, social characteristics frequently entered women's decisions. In the extract that follows, Marie describes the personality characteristics that were important to her and her partner. The conceptualization of these personality traits indicates that these women want a shared affinity with the child, but also that they regard these characteristics to be, in some way, genetically inheritable. If they believed musical ability and athleticism to be the result of one's environment and nurturing, then the likely scenario would be that their influence as parents could lead to a child's interest and, thus, abilities in sports and music. Nonetheless, these women give credence to the belief that nature and, thus, biology, influence musical and athletic traits: "I was looking for somebody that had music as one of their interests. My partner wanted somebody with athletic interests or, or some of the same things that she shares, some of, perhaps athletic or other things." Although the biological determinism inherent in these constructions is apparent, so, too, are the women's desires to share affinities with the potential offspring. In this case, Marie's partner expressed a desire for the donor to share social characteristics with her. Similarly, although, Janella attests to the belief that personalities are not only something you are born with but also something that is inheritable, her comments express her and her partner's desire for shared subjectivities with the donor, and, possibly by extension, the potential child:

> Even though we didn't know the person, any sign at all about what the person was like felt really important. So like anybody who seemed really uptight or something, we thought, 'cause you know what I mean? [laughing] They're born with a personality. You have some influence, but . . . We thought, well, it would be good to also feel like because . . . you know . . . I mean they're kind of like an imaginary person. Their personality is imaginary. So if you think the person is kind of a nice person, it's nicer to think about it.

As these quotes indicate, respondents frequently mentioned selecting donors based on personality characteristics such as "niceness" and "decency"; social characteristics such as "well educated"; and physical characteristics such as being "athletic," strong, or in excellent health. The following statement by

Janella illustrates the ways in which women consider a range of factors when selecting a sperm donor.

> After selecting based on Hispanic and Caucasian, we tried to get somebody athletic and well educated. They also had to seem nice. In their personal profiles, they had to seem like decent people. Not too freaked out or Type A, you know. Those were the biggest things.

All of these characteristics are listed on the sperm bank donor profiles provided to their clients, and it is not surprising that women prioritized these attributes and made decisions based on them. What is interesting, however, is the meanings these attributes held for the women making these selections. Affinity includes aspects beyond appearance and encompasses social and cultural characteristics such as national origin, religious ancestry, cultural interests, hobbies, and social characteristics. Although these are not known to be genetically hereditary traits, they are nonetheless significant to women's choices for their power to construct relatedness based on relational and biological connection.

Conclusion

This chapter highlights key aspects of the achieving pregnancy for lesbians: finding and choosing sperm and constructing affinity ties. In these stories, initial articulations of deliberate and conscious planning emerge. Women consciously get ready, gather information, embark on a "sperm hunt," and construct notions of relatedness that fit their needs. Flexibility is necessary as women negotiate achieving pregnancy processes, and they frequently revise their plans. For example, for those women who were unable or later chose not to use a known donor, semen banks became sources for semen. Here, women must select a donor from catalogs provided by sperm banks. A central idea that emerges throughout women's experiences with semen selection is the sense that donor selection and the consideration of characteristics are performed, in the words of one respondent, "because you can." This significantly highlights the importance of the institutional organization of assisted reproduction and the organization of consumption via catalogs.

For all the women interviewed, the one indisputable known factor was that the sperm would not originate from their primary partners. Processes of obtaining sperm are varied, and the spectrum of "choices" creates potentially transformative possibilities. As Weston (1991) so well describes, for gay and lesbian people, families are more about choice than sanctioned legal and blood ties.

Donor selection emphasizes shared social and cultural affinities with the potential parents. As such, affinity ties are also significant to the creation and maintenance of social legitimacy for lesbian families. Affinity ties provide legitimacy in the context of uncertain legal rights and heteronormativity. Although these ideas are implied in all donor decisions, nowhere is it more illustrative than in cases of donor selection from sperm banks. As women interact with sperm banks, they manipulate and construct ideal donors and ideal children. Thus, from a sociological perspective, processes of achieving pregnancy among lesbians reveal that relatedness itself is a constructed phenomenon.

References

Associated Press (2002), Founder of sperm-donor internet site says he's overwhelmed by response. Accessed on June 26, 2002. Available at www.intelihealth.com.

Clarke, A. E. & Fujimura, J. H. (1992), *The Right Tools for the Job: At Work in Twentieth Century Life Sciences*. Princeton, NJ: Princeton University Press.

—— Shim, J., Mamo, L., Fosket, J. R. & Fishman, J. R. (2003), Biomedicalization: Theorizing technoscientific transformations of health, illness, and U.S. biomedicine. *Amer. Sociol. Rev.*, 68:161–194.

Jetter, A. (1996), Lesbian baby boom. *Harper's Bazaar*, October, pp. 66–70.

Kendell, K., with Haaland, R., eds. (1996), *Lesbians Choosing Motherhood: Legal Implications of Donor Insemination, Second Parent Adoption, Co-Parenting, Ovum Donation and Embryo Transfer*. San Francisco: National Center for Lesbian Rights.

Kolata, G. (2002), Fertility inc.: Clinics race to lure clients. *The New York Times*, January 1, pp. D1, D7.

Mamo, L. (2002), Sexuality, reproduction, and biomedical nego-
    tiations: An analysis of achieving pregnancy in the absence
    of heterosexuality. Unpublished doctoral dissertation,
    Department of Social and Behavioral Sciences, University
    of California, San Francisco.
Saffron, L. (1994), *Challenging Conceptions: Planning a Family by
    Self-Insemination.* London: Cassell.
Schmidt, M. & Moore, L. J. (1998), Constructing a "good catch,"
    picking a winner: The development of technosemen and
    the deconstruction of the monolithic male. In: *Cyborg
    Babies: From Techno-Sex to Techno-Tots*, ed. R. Davis-Floyd &
    J. Dumit. New York: Routledge, pp. 21–39.
Weston, K. (1991), *Families We Choose: Lesbians, Gays, Kinship.*
    New York: Columbia University Press.

8

Passion, Play, and Erotic Potential Space in Lesbian Relationships

Suzanne Iasenza

The only shame I ever feel now, after so many years of women's touch, is never saying thank you enough.

— Joan Nestle, *A Fragile Union*

How well do present psychoanalytic theories guide us in how to cocreate and maintain safe erotic environments for lesbian women? Several feminist, social constructionist, and postmodern psychoanalytic works, some of which use relational and intersubjective perspectives, are promising in their attempts to identify and break down pathologizing sex and gender dichotomies and hierarchies that characterized earlier theory and practice (Benjamin, 1988; O'Connor and Ryan, 1993; Chodorow, 1994; Glassgold and Iasenza, 1995; Burch, 1997; Magee and Miller, 1997; Schwartz, 1998; Lesser and Schoenberg, 1999; Gould and Kiersky, 2001). Additionally, the acceptance of openly lesbian psychoanalysts as clinicians, teachers, and supervisors in many psychoanalytic communities creates opportunities for more diverse and inclusive discussions of these issues (Martin, 1995; Crespi, 2001).

We are now in a position to examine deeper levels of transferences to theory that raise complex issues. For example, what is problematic about our love affair with the new gay and lesbian affirmative psychoanalytic discourse, most of which is based on postmodernism and queer theory's mission to abolish sex and gender categories? A major problem is that it obscures the particularities of women's sexual subjectivities, especially the continuing influences of sexism and misogyny in many women's erotic lives. A different and opposite problem is that in our attempts to counteract the pathologizing of lesbian sexuality, we sometimes rely too heavily on gender socialization theories that characterize lesbian relationships as doubly burdened by female sexual socialization, paradoxically overgeneralizing and essentializing lesbian behavior in ways similar to classical theory (see Iasenza, 2000, for a more thorough discussion of this problem as it relates to the development of the "lesbian bed death" concept). Where are the rich and complex stories about lesbian sexual relating in psychoanalytic literature? As a psychodynamically oriented sex therapist, my search has been a frustrating one. So many presentations and publications about "lesbian sexuality" wind up desexualizing lesbian relating by focusing on sexual identity or object relations rather than actual sexual fantasies, desires, or behaviors. The proliferation of gay and lesbian affirmative perspectives begins the process of creating safe psychoanalytic communities within which clinical experiences with lesbian sexuality may be explored. This chapter is one contribution toward this effort as it presents a relational lesbian-affirmative approach in working with lesbian couples who identify sexual difficulties as their major challenge. The case material illustrates how analysis of dreams and erotic transference–countertransference may promote passion, play, and the cocreation of erotic potential space within which lesbian couples may develop sexual agency and entitlement.

Let's Talk About Sex — *Really*
"Sexuality is alive and well and living in psychoanalysis. You just have to know where to look for it," asserts Muriel Dimen (1999, p. 415), and she is right. A search for lesbian psychoanalytic sex stories reveals some "hidden treasures." Beverly Burch (1993) offers descriptions of "gender devices and desires" that some lesbian partners use to play with real or imagined gen-

dered sexual selves. These devices involve a fluidity of masculinity and femininity, sexual passivity and activity. For example, one couple she interviewed stated,

> MIRIAM: I love it when she's "femmed up." It's a real sexual turn-on.
> ELLEN: Miriam would really like us both out in public in heels with nylons.
> MIRIAM: It's the idea of being physical with somebody who's really dressed like a woman. Then this is really lesbian! This is two women! I mean pantyhose and everything! It's a real turn-on to me. The idea of being in a restaurant and sliding my hand under her skirt and over her silky pantyhose. Wow! [p. 117].

In this passionate moment, sameness, not complementarity, is the basis of sexual turn-on and femininity is associated with sexual activity, the sliding of a desiring hand under a skirt. The playful use of clothing here is reminiscent of D'Ercole's (1996) image of sex and gender constructs as a "variable wardrobe of postures and poses worn and discarded as the fashion and context change" (p. 143).

A couple of treasured examples of lesbian erotics in the therapeutic context can also found in the literature (Deutsch, 1995; Kiersky, 1996). Both Deutsch and Kiersky convey vulnerable passionate analytic moments when female analysts made crucial choices about how to handle erotic dreams and erotic transference–countertransference phenomena. In Deutsch's account a lesbian patient, Ava, dreamed the following: "I am in a museum. There is a huge 10-foot painting of 2 graces holding hands. I was standing, looking at it and one of them walked out of the painting, into the room. I looked at her" (p. 35).

Ava experienced the dream as "very soothing, very voluptuous" and believed it represented an acceptance of her own and other women's beauty, as she remembered her mother calling her and her two sisters the Three Graces.

Her recognition of her own and other women's beauty was expressed to the analyst in the form of a fantasy in which Ava said she is "three or four years old and wants to go under her [the analyst's] skirt, lift it up, and kiss her" (p. 35). The analyst, whom Deutsch (1995) identifies as heterosexual, received Ava's sexual longings in a loving way, acknowledging not only her (the analyst's) preoedipal role as nurturing mother but also her oedipal role as sexual object, and accepted Ava's sexual desire "like a gift," a response that enabled Ava to move beyond romantic splits and conflicts in her life as her love for women and herself was affirmed.

How lucky Ava was to have found such a conscious and secure analyst who could stay the course of being sexual object for her lesbian patient. How did the sexual subjectivity of the analyst play a role? Was it easier to stay the course because she was heterosexually identified? Is staying the course easiest when a patient's erotic strivings are presented (or are understood) as emanating from childhood years (Davies, 1998)? Glassgold (1995) asserts that therapists, of any sexual orientation, must accept being not only the object but also the subject of homoerotic desire in order for the patient to experience sexual agency and individuation.

Kiersky's (1996) patient, having survived many years in emotional exile as a woman who sexually desires other women, struggled to integrate a new narrative, offered by Kiersky, that her same-sex childhood, adolescent, and adult sexual longings and desires were acceptable and normal. A moving example of an erotic therapeutic moment was in an interchange in which the patient, Kate, expressed feelings of closeness and recognition that Kiersky did, in fact, care about her. Kiersky reports that within this context Kate fell silent and then said, "You know, you did turn in the last session to write an appointment for me, you may not remember, but your skirt slipped up and I saw a lot of your leg. I wondered if you were aware of it?" Kiersky responded, "Did you wonder if I was being seductive with you?" (p. 139).

Kiersky, in that moment, not only mirrors her patient's sexual desire as acceptable and real, but introduces herself as a sexual agent, one who is capable of seducing her patient. This opens up the potential for Kate to further embrace and develop her own sexual subjectivity through a positive sexual identification with the analyst. More important, as Kate later says, Kiersky's question makes her realize how Kiersky's seduction of her is *imaginable*, that she (Kate) realizes she is attractive enough for Kiersky (an Other) to want to seduce her.

In the mother–child relationship, Winnicott discusses the importance of the development of "potential space in which, because of trust, the child may creatively play" (1971, p. 109). Sustaining safe erotic potential spaces for lesbian patients requires a conscious decision by the therapist to discard traditional psychoanalytic notions of lesbian desire and sexual expression as infantile, abnormal, and unreal (Iasenza, 1995; Kiersky, 1996). Instead, the therapist and patient cocreate a safe erotic therapeutic environment where the patient may trust the therapist to mirror her lesbian desires as healthy and mature, freeing her to explore sexual passion and play creatively. The complexities of cocreating safe erotic potential space with lesbian couples is illustrated in the following case material.

The Erotic Couple Context
The most common presenting sexual problems for lesbian couples fall into three overlapping categories (in no particular order). The first is difficulty accepting sexual differences (in sexual preferences, in levels of desire, in sexual styles). The second is infrequent or unfulfilling sex due to life stresses such as work pressures, trying to have or raise children, physical or mental health issues in selves or significant others, the impact of menopause and aging, the emotional and physical effects of medications, and issues surrounding death and loss. The third is sexual disruptions and distortions due to the often-devastating impact of incest, child physical or emotional abuse (including the effects of homophobia and misogyny), or sexual assault. Partners may agree or disagree about these issues, feel justified about their own position, blame the other, feel damaged, rejected, shamed, or confused. Often, by the time they enter sex therapy, the partners have cocreated an antierotic environment where mistrust, withdrawal, or defensiveness prevents any possibility of the expansiveness and surrender that characterize passionate or playful interactions.

The goal of treatment is to help the couple (re)create an erotic environment in which they may explore, expand, and enjoy their sexual potential. Through the use of a combination of behavioral and educational interventions (homework assignments) and psychodynamic interpretations, the couple may discover the conscious and unconscious childhood events, couple dynamics, and societal influences that contribute to sexual conflict and may begin to identify, appreciate, and incorporate individual sexual styles (Masters and Johnson, 1970; Kaplan, 1974). Having good sex often mobilizes guilt and anxiety about boundary maintenance, comfort with intimacy, body image, religious and family attitudes about sex, and feelings of worthiness. Lesbian women may face additional doses of sexual guilt, fear, anxiety, and shame if they feel that they are enjoying sex too much within societal or familial systems that repress both female sexuality and lesbian behavior (Buloff and Osterman, 1995; Gair, 1995).

Therapists have the opportunity to play an important role in the revitalization of their patients' sexual lives by cocreating the potential space to work and play with the motivations and resistances that make up erotic life. They serve as sex educator, role model, transferential object, and coach. An out lesbian therapist can be, especially for lesbian patients, the good sexual mother they never had, who accepts their love and desire for other women, who maintains good boundaries, and who acts as nonjudgmental coach. Brown (1993), in working with lesbian couples, reminds therapists of the need to be aware of how their own internalized homophobia and attitudes about genital sexual activity influence the therapy.

Additionally, therapists have inherited, consciously or unconsciously, a psychoanalytic legacy that is relevant here, namely, Freud's (1905) privileging of the vaginal orgasm. In his configuration of dual erotogenic zones, the clitoris and the vagina, Freud set up a false dichotomy of female sexual experience in which clitoral play represents early infantile sexuality and the vaginal orgasm is considered to be the hallmark of mature normal female development (Kaplan, 1974). We now know, as Kaplan points out, through Masters and Johnson's (1966, 1970) landmark studies that women experience one orgasm which has both clitoral and vaginal components.

Freud privileged not only the vaginal orgasm but also genital sexuality in general as the goal of mature sexual development. This belief, maintained in society in general, in the mental health community, and in the lesbian community, has contributed to the pathologizing of lesbian women, who prefer little or no genital sex (Rothblum and Brehony, 1993) or those who don't experience orgasm. Loulan's work (1984) is especially helpful in counteracting the prescriptive genital and orgasmic sexual script by making pleasure (however achieved) rather than orgasm the goal of sexual activity.

Ruth and Lucy: The Cocreation of Erotic Play and Passion

Ruth and Lucy entered sex therapy to explore why they hadn't had satisfactory sexual relations for the last half of their 12-year relationship. Both were angry — Ruth because she felt frustrated by Lucy's "no's" to sex over the years, and Lucy because she felt attacked and blamed by Ruth for their sexual problems. Therapy initially focused on helping them define the problem, reduce blame, and enhance the erotic environment in the relationship.

One of their first homework assignments was to view a Betty Dodson (1991) video, *Self-Loving*, about a group sexuality seminar in which 10 naked women, aged 28 to 60, explore sexual self-pleasure including examining and appreciating their genitals and learning how to increase orgasmic potential using breathing techniques, different positions, pelvic movements, and electric vibrators. Educational videos are commonly used in sex therapy especially for women (Tiefer, 1996). They are used in psychodynamically-oriented sex therapy not only to educate but also to stimulate discussion that often reveals intrapsychic and interpersonal conflicts. Because this couple entered treatment in such an angry, other-blaming state, I selected Dodson's masturbation video intentionally to begin identifying how each individual woman's sexuality was contributing to the couple's sexual dynamics.

Dodson teaches about and participates in sexual activity in an authoritative yet playful way, all the while advocating that women be responsible for their own sexual pleasure. Ruth and Lucy's reactions to viewing such a variety of ordinary women so open to their bodies and sexuality included an intense dialogue about their shame and self-consciousness about their bodies, weight, being naked, and certain sexual acts. Lucy wondered why she hadn't penetrated herself at all while masturbating: "What's my block?" Ruth expressed amazement that women would do such a thing as participating in this video, especially women who had children. She likened the group to a witch's coven, engaged in the taboo of women owning their sexual powers — a dangerous act that thrilled yet terrified her.

Both Ruth and Lucy recalled painful childhood memories involving parental criticisms and intrusiveness that compromised their senses of body and sexual integrity. As we worked through their feelings of shame, fear, and anger, sexual spontaneity resurfaced — along with a playfulness and passion that reactivated an intense genital sexuality they had experienced earlier in their relationship but had later lost. Lucy expressed concern about her lifelong difficulty enjoying penetrative sex (sometimes not even being able to bear inserting one of her own fingers inside herself) because she associated it with a way that men dominated women, something she had resisted her whole life. We began deconstructing her belief about the oppressive nature of penetration, which unleashed years of repressed rage she felt at witnessing the gender indignities her mother, her sisters, and female friends suffered at the hands of men. She became increasingly aware of her own struggles for respect as one of the few women executives within a male-dominated profession, leading her to make some long overdue changes at work.

Lucy's concern about penetration transformed into a desire for Ruth to enter her and she (Lucy) was amazed at the depth of her yearning to receive and be filled. The ensuing months of treatment contained reports of intense mutual genital sexuality including genital stimulation with tongues and fingers, as well as penetration with fingers, hands, and dildos.

Penetrability and Masculine Identification
As Ruth and Lucy processed the meanings and feelings connected to this period of intense genital activity, Lucy brought in this dream:

I come into our therapy session and look down to see that I have these long inner lips down to my knees. I'm astounded. I feel uncomfortable because I told you something that was incorrect. My inner labia were much longer than I originally reported to you. They would swing to and fro when I walked.

Lucy was excited but embarrassed to share this dream. I was receptive upon hearing it, attributing it (in my head) to her expansion into receptive penetrative sex and her increased comfort with the feminine as an empowering part of her body and sexual psyche. I visually imagined her imposing swollen vulva to be a welcomed addition to Judy Chicago's "Dinner Party," a 1970s feminist art exhibit that displayed a dinner table where place settings of famous women in history consisted of sculpted plates whose vulva-like contours expanded in size as women's "places" in history grew.

Imagine my surprise at hearing Lucy's associations to her dream. She associated her "large swinging labia" with the freedom and strength in her body that she last experienced as a tomboy in childhood. She remembered dressing and looking so much like a boy that most people mistook her for one. She masturbated often then, felt connected to her body, including her genitals, and felt there was no limit to what she could do, competing and winning in games with boys as well as girls. She identified the beginnings of her belief in the intrusiveness of receptive genital sex as coinciding with her having to relinquish her beloved tomboy identity upon entering young womanhood.

For Lucy, it was this recovered masculine (tomboy) identification, as represented by her "large swinging labia," an overt public bulging genital and personal entitlement, that allowed her to embrace an active, powerful feminine genital receptivity with her lover. Additionally while being penetrated more at home, she became more penetrating at work. Lucy deconstructs the dichotomies of gender and sexuality (penetrative–penetrable, active–passive, feminine–masculine) and recombines aspects of each, reminding us of the fluid nature of multiple identifications and sexual desires (Benjamin, 1988; Dimen, 1991; Harris, 1991; Elise, 1998).

Although she at first presented her dream and associations tentatively Lucy grew more certain and even celebratory in sharing her experience as Ruth and I listened and supported the integration of her identities and erotic desires. Ruth, too, experienced a healing in feeling more sexually desirable, wanted, as Lucy openly expressed her desire for Ruth to enter her.

The Therapist as the Erotic Third

"It is this [oedipal] third that paradoxically provides both the freedom for the flames of passion and romantic idealization to burn so brightly and a horizon to its expression and reach" (Cooper, 1998, p. 771). This is how Cooper characterizes the analyst's symbolic role in his commentary on Davies's (1998) paper on erotic transference and countertransference. Sweetnam (1999) refers to the "erotic third" as an unconscious intersubjectivity created within couple dyads that promotes the development of gender transformations in the partners.

Therapists play various transference roles with couples as part of the therapeutic triad, cocreating the contexts for passions and transformations as well as constructing the boundaries that keep a safe horizon in sight. Some transferences that ordinarily would be analyzed and worked through in individual therapy are instead "encouraged and exploited in the service of [sex therapy] treatment . . . [like the omnipotent parent who has] . . . the power to give them permission to engage in 'forbidden' activities, to pronounce moral judgments" (Kaplan, 1974, p. 242). This intentional sex-affirmative parental role that Kaplan advocated for heterosexual couples was used to counteract sex-negative familial and cultural messages that inhibit adult (hetero)sexual relating. This role can be expanded when working with lesbian couples to include lesbian-affirmative messages to counteract both female-negative and homo-negative childhood sexual messages. For example, my messages to Ruth and Lucy that masturbation is good, that it's okay to ask for the sex you want, that lesbian desire is wonderful, delivered within a (parental) therapeutic role, created the safety for them to identify and work through some of the guilt, shame, and fear that was instilled in them by childhood parental figures.

Other common transferences are the idealized Good (sexual) Mother (the one who nurtures their sexual selves, promotes sexual pride, and mirrors same-sex desire), the Authoritarian Mother (who gives them homework, holds expectations for their performance, can give or take away praise), the Oedipal Competitor ("You like her better, find her more attractive, give her more A's than me"), and the Erotic Mother (the one who sexually has it all, is the sexual subject extraordinaire, who inspires sexual envy and competition, who the patient desires as sexual and love object).

Sex therapy requires an open discussion of sexually related material — patients' behaviors, desires, and fantasies — that may accelerate the development of erotic transference and countertransference. The presence of the therapist as an erotic third often permits partners to reveal passions and play that remained dormant in the dyadic relationship. The presence of one or the other patient as witness at any given time may assist the therapist in containing and exploring intense levels of discursive erotics that often surface as the therapeutic endeavor deepens.

The Use of the Therapist's Body

Lucy's "labia dream" is an excellent example of how people's deepest losses, yearnings, and pleasures are written on or in the body. Her dream and associations to it gave voice to an integration process of body and psyche that was central to her erotic life with Ruth. In the course of treatment, especially when erotic transferences surface, the patient's dreams and fantasies may involve parts of the therapist's body as well. If the therapist can contain and permit such usage patients may be able to articulate the intersubjective experiences that contribute to their sexual senses of self. After the "labia dream," Lucy brought in an essay she had written about me that Ruth agreed she should share with me since it contained particular meanings for Ruth as well. The essay, titled, "Suzanne's Breasts," went as follows:

> I felt like exploding when I entered the room. My eyes were filled with Suzanne's breasts which seemed to couch her smiling face. I was immediately fearful that I would catch Ruth's eye and laugh out loud from the terror of my reaction. I was also enjoying my desire and as the meeting progressed transformed the feeling into the air and felt all three of us were engaged together in a swaying mass of softness. I had to work hard to listen as I was busy letting my eyes feel so glad.

Both Lucy and Ruth seemed to enjoy the writing of the essay and the thought of sharing it with me. I asked them to talk more about their associations to my breasts, their attractions, fantasies, wishes, and fears. Lucy first focused on how she loved the large size of my breasts, reminding her of a beloved nanny she had had (and abruptly lost) who soothed her by letting her fall asleep with her head lying on her large breasts. She was devastated by her nanny's unexplained disappearance, which also reminded her about how little nurturing she received from her alcoholic mother. Her yearning for closeness with her mother was still a palpable presence in her life.

Ruth emphasized her yearning for love and friendship with me, how she and Lucy especially appreciated my attention and support of them as lesbian women, something neither of them received from their mothers who they described as "boy moms," mothers who gave preferential treatment to the boys in the family. Subsequent discussions about my breasts involved Lucy's fantasies about what she'd like to do to me or have me do to her sexually. Ruth denied having sexual feelings of her own initially because they felt "too incestuous." She related to me (and yearned to have me) most as the sister she never had in her life. Ruth needed a much longer time to reveal her erotic transference, to trust that I wouldn't reject her body and sexuality the way her father did.

Much of the working through of the erotic tranferences involved re-experiencing the suffering of past abandonments and attacks, expressing disappointments and anger about our relationship, and acknowledging the erotic tension and loving feelings in the room. My breasts were part of an ongoing conversation with which I learned to be comfortable, trusting that Ruth and Lucy knew on some level where they needed to go with the subject. A colleague once asked me after hearing about this process, "Wasn't all the talk about your breasts a challenge? How did you deal with such heat?" Upon reflection I realized that much of the discussion of my breasts felt containable, perhaps because I am, as a woman in this culture, used to attention on (my) breasts. A much "hotter" moment, revealed by my blushing, was an interchange with Ruth in which she said, "You know what my favorite part of your body is? It's the area right near your left temple, slightly under your brow. I love how that part looks. That's the sexiest part of your body." I blushed, she noticed, and in that moment I felt more exposed and seen than in many of our breast conversations. I realized how so much of eroticism is alive in those felt moments of recognition (Benjamin, 1995).

Most of the time I was able to maintain a lightness and humor about being used as sexual object. This, I later learned, provided significant healing for Lucy and Ruth given their histories of sexual repression and shame. I experienced many difficult countertransference moments as well, however, including feelings of vulnerability, concerns about maintaining appropriate boundaries, and grief over my own (sexual) losses that were triggered during our therapeutic process. One example of such a countertransference moment was when we discussed ending therapy. In response to their expressions of how special I was and the ways I'd been there for them, I asked, "What do you think you could do to replace me?" They swiftly called me on this remark, forcing me to examine my attempt to minimize their loss and my own feelings of grief about saying good-bye.

The Breast as Metaphor

Ruth and Lucy's use of my breasts changed over the years. Both of them eventually moved away from my body, talking less about my breasts. My breasts, when referred to, served more as metaphor, about connection, about playfulness, and about trust. Having made our way through the heat and hurts, the passion and play, Ruth and Lucy were able to articulate what they felt was the most helpful part of our work together. They said that they loved the way I would talk about my breasts in humorous ways because it made them feel that I trusted them to keep good boundaries. They loved how real I was with them, that I acknowledged how I missed them when they were away, and how they had an impact on me in the relationship. The breast became our symbol, real and metaphorical, of a cocreated process of mutuality and recognition that involved expressions of pain, passion, and play.

Conclusion

A relational frame permits the exploration of multiple meanings of erotic dreams and transference as well as acknowledging and exploring the therapist's countertransference. Sexual feelings, fantasies, wishes, and fears are understood within a context in which we view "transference–countertransference as intrinsically and irreducibly interactive" (Davies, 1999, p. 185).

Finally, when working on sexual concerns, therapists should incorporate a lesbian-affirmative stance in which antifemale and antilesbian familial and cultural messages are identified and deconstructed, this will allow patients to acknowledge and work through feelings of invisibility, shame, and humiliation. The lesbian-affirmative therapeutic context helps the therapist and couple cocreate the erotic potential space within which couples may recover or discover the passions and play in their erotic life.

References

Benjamin, J. (1988), The Bonds of Love. London: Virago.
—— (1995), Like Subjects, Love Objects. New Haven, CT: Yale University Press.
Brown, L. S. (1993), The boston marriage in the therapy office. In: Boston Marriages: Romantic But Asexual Relationships Among Lesbians, ed. D. Rothblum & K. A. Brehony. Amherst: University of Massachusetts Press, pp. 86–95.
Buloff, B. & Osterman, M. (1995), Queer reflections: Mirroring and the lesbian experience of self. In: Lesbians and Psychoanalysis: Revolutions in Theory and Practice, ed. J. M. Glassgold & S. Iasenza. New York: Free Press, pp. 93–106.
Burch, B. (1993), On Intimate Terms: The Psychology of Difference in Lesbian Relationships. Urbana: University of Illinois Press.
—— (1997), Other Women: Lesbian/Bisexual Experience and Psychoanalytic Views of Women. New York: Columbia University Press.
Chodorow, N. J. (1994), Femininities, Masculinities, Sexualities: Freud and Beyond. Lexington: University of Kentucky Press.
Cooper, S. H. (1998), Flirting, post-oedipus, and mutual protectiveness in the analytic dyad: Commentary on paper by Jody Messler Davies. Psychoanal. Dial., 8:767–779.
Crespi, L. (2001), From baby boom to gayby boom: Twenty-five years of psychoanalysis in the lesbian community. In: Sexualities Lost and Found, ed. E. Gould & S. Kiersky. Madison, CT: International Universities Press, pp. 261–275.
Davies, J. M. (1998), Between the disclosure and foreclosure of

erotictransference–countertransference: Can psychoanalysis
find a place for adult sexuality? *Psychoanal. Dial.*, 8:747–766.
———— (1999), Getting cold feet, defining "safe-enough" bor-
ders: Dissociation, multiplicity, and integration in the ana-
lyst's experience. *Psychoanal. Quart.*, 68: 184–208.
D'Ercole, A. (1996), Postmodern ideas about gender and sexuality: The lesbian woman redundancy. *Psychoanal. &
Psychother.*, 13:142–152.
Deutsch, L. (1995), Out of the closet and on to the couch: A psy-
cho-analytic exploration of lesbian development. In:
*Lesbians and Psychoanalysis: Revolutions in Theory and
Practice*, ed. J. M. Glassgold & S. Iasenza. New York: Free
Press, pp. 19–37.
Dimen, M. (1991), Deconstructing difference: Gender, splitting
and transitional space. *Psychoanal. Dial.*, 1:335–352.
———— (1999), Between lust and libido: Sex, psychoanalysis, and
the moment before. *Psychoanal. Dial.*, 9:415–440.
Dodson, B. (1991), Self-loving: Portrait of a women's sexuality
semi-nar [video]. Available at www.Bettydodson.com.
Elise, D. (1998), Gender repertoire: Body, mind, and bisexuality.
Psychoanal. Dial., 8:353–371.
Freud, S. (1905), Three essays on the theory of sexuality. *Standard
Edition*, 7:130–243, London: Hogarth Press, 1953.
Gair, S. R. (1995), The false self, shame, and the challenge of self-
cohesion. In: *Lesbians and Psychoanalysis: Revolutions in
Theory and Practice,* ed. J. M. Glassgold & S. Iasenza. New
York: Free Press, pp. 107–123.
Glassgold, J. M. (1995), Psychoanalysis with lesbians: Self-reflec-
tion and agency. In: *Lesbians and Psychoanalysis: Revolutions
in Theory and Practice,* ed. J. M. Glassgold & S. Iasenza. New
York: Free Press, pp. 203–228.
Glassgold, J. M. & Iasenza, S., eds. (1995), *Lesbians and
Psychoanalysis: Revolutions in Theory and Practice.* New York:
Free Press.
Gould, E. & Kiersky, S., eds. (2001), *Sexualities Lost and Found:
Lesbians, Psychoanalysis, and Culture.* Madison, CT:
International Universities Press.
Harris, A. (1991), In fact she was a feminist: Gender as contra-
diction. *Psychoanal. Dial.*, 1:197–225.

Iasenza, S. (1995), Platontic pleasures and dangerous desires: Psychoanalytic theory, sex research, and lesbian sexuality. In: *Lesbians and Psychoanalysis: Revolutions in Theory and Practice*, ed. J. M. Glassgold & S. Iasenza. New York: Free Press, pp. 345–373.

—— (2000), Lesbian sexuality post-Stonewall to postmodernism: Putting the "lesbian bed death" concept to bed. *J. Sex Ed. & Ther.*, 25:59–69.

Kaplan, H. S. (1974), *The New Sex Therapy.* New York: Brunner/Mazel.

Kiersky, S. (1996), Exiled desire: The problem of reality in psychoanalysis and lesbian experience. *Psychoanal. & Psychother.*, 13:130–141.

Lesser, R. C. & Schoenberg, E., eds. (1999), *That Obscure Subject of Desire.* New York: Routledge.

Loulan, J. (1984), *Lesbian Sex.* Duluth, MN: Spinsters Ink.

Magee, M. & Miller, D. C. (1997), *Lesbian Lives: Psychoanalytic Narratives Old and New.* Hillsdale, NJ: The Analytic Press.

Martin, A. (1995), A view from both sides: Coming out as a lesbian psychoanalyst. In: *Disorienting Sexuality*, ed. T. Domenici & R. C. Lesser. New York: Routledge, pp. 255–261.

Masters, W. H. & Johnson, V. E. (1966), *Human Sexual Response.* Boston: Little, Brown.

———— (1970), *Human Sexual Inadequacy.* Boston: Little, Brown.

O'Connor, N. & Ryan, J. (1993), *Wild Desires and Mistaken Identities: Lesbianism and Psychoanalysis.* New York: Columbia University Press.

Rothblum, E. D. & Brehony, K. A., eds. (1993), *Boston Marriages: Romantic but Asexual Relationships Among Lesbians.* Amherst: University of Massachusetts Press.

Schwartz, A. (1998), *Sexual Subjects: Lesbians, Gender and Psychoanalysis.* New York: Routledge.

Sweetnam, A. (1999), Sexual sensations and gender experience: The psychological positions and the erotic third. *Psychoanal. Dial.*, 9:327–348.

Tiefer, L. (1996), Towards a feminist sex therapy. In: *Sexualities*, ed. M. Hall. New York: Harrington Park Press, pp. 53–64.

Winnicott, D. W. (1971), *Playing and Reality.* London: Tavistock.

9

One Plus One Equals One
Money Matters in Same-Sex Relationships

Barbra Zuck Locker

oney is a hot topic. Money and sex. Money and power. Money is often linked with highly charged subjects and it is, in itself, highly charged. No one is neutral about money. Everyone has feelings about it.

Talking about money is difficult for all couples, gay and straight. In a 1999 piece written for the *New Yorker*, cultural critic Daphne Merkin tells of her schizophrenic experience growing up in a very wealthy family that was extremely ambivalent about money. Secrecy and shame about money pervaded family life. She provides a telling example of how parental attitudes toward money shape children's behaviors. Merkin admits that as an adult, she remains confused, concerned and somewhat blinded around money. She attributes the breakup of her marriage to financial misunderstandings and to her own inability to deal with them. In her astute social commentary, Merkin (1999) observes the following:

> For all of the loosening up that the eighties brought, money remains quite firmly in the closet. . . . We don't really tell each other very much. The simple truth is that I haven't the vaguest idea what kind of money even my closest friends live on. . . . My friends, I might add, can't have a much better idea of how I make ends meet [pp. 94-96].

Merkin's account poignantly illustrates how one's personal relationships with money often remain out of awareness and how one can bring assumptions, expectations, and conflicts about finances into relationships with others, particularly one's spouse or partners. Money issues in couples reflect many aspects of the relationship, including each partner's sense of self and feelings about the other.

Although the emotional impact of economic issues can be staggering, the many meanings of money are not a central focus of the psychoanalytic literature. Do analysts, like their patients, avoid the subject? Lieberman and Lindner (1987) coined the term "moneyblindness" to describe a tendency to deny money's value and place in human interactions. One might assume that anxiety is the basis for such avoidance both for analysts and for their patients. One indication that money may be the last taboo (Mellan, 1992) is seen in the consulting room, where patients who are likely to give vivid details of their most intimate sexual encounters are somewhat coy about the exact amount of an annual bonus. Yet analysts are always learning about their patients and themselves by the ways in which fees are negotiated and handled (Liss-Levinson, 1990). How money is managed in treatment is often highly revealing of an individual's or couple's capacity for intimacy. In couples treatment, listening to how the pair deals with money can yield valuable information about many other aspects of the relationship.

Money will inevitably have some symbolic meaning in a relationship; each relationship generates its own meanings based on the individual and joint experiences of the members of the couple. Money is both a personal and interpersonal issue. It is a common ingredient in self-definition and is almost always a tie that binds, both in families and in couples. Couples argue about money, use it to control or blackmail and even to exploit each other. They also dream together, share fantasies and aspirations for the future, and make plans, many of which are dependent on financial conditions as yet unknown. Most dreams come with a price tag. Working out how the price is paid and by whom can be a thorny process in many relationships. For many couples — gay and straight — reaching consensus about money issues requires enormous effort over an extended period of time.

An inability to manage financial issues may restrict intimacy and foster isolation within a couple. Alternately, a couple's capacity to share money may be indicative of the two people's ability to share a life. That is not to say that resources must be pooled equally in all marriages, but partnerships are enhanced when couples know how to resolve financial conflicts in an open, honest way. At the very least, couples need to be able to resolve these differences in a way that works for them.

Money issues are not unique to same-sex couples. In clinical practice I have not observed any notable differences in the way gay and straight patients handle money in their relationships. Sociocultural and legal factors, however, as well as gender-role expectations, have a different impact on same-sex couples than they do on their straight counterparts. This can affect the meanings that are attached to money. For example, in same-sex couples, the organization of financial matters will inevitably raise questions in each partner's mind about the ways in which each partner is conforming to or deviating from stereotypical gender roles. Both may have feelings and opinions about the financial gender role they are playing and about the part their partner is playing. This can make it difficult, although not impossible, for same-sex couples to negotiate financial intimacy. It also contributes to what I call "mathematical madness," or the multiplicity of ways in which couples use money to avoid closeness and how financial issues, like sexual ones, come to symbolize other problems in a relationship. This chapter explores the functions that money plays in the life of some same-sex couples. Although it focuses primarily on same-sex pairs, many of the observations can be applied to all couples.

Same-Sex Couples and Money

When comparing how gay and lesbian versus straight couples deal with money issues, there is always a tendency to drift into discussions of legal and social policies that create inequities between those who can marry and those who cannot. These realities are profound, and they do affect the role that money plays in same-sex pairs. In heterosexual marriage, there is an assumption of financial mutuality, or economic equality, although patterns of dealing with money vary widely from marriage to marriage. Two legally married people have to work against this premise with legally defined prenuptial agreements to "unshare." In homosexual "marriages," the law makes it necessary to work actively toward creating mutuality and to merge finances actively or protect one partner in case of the other's death or disability.

In addition to the legal and social-policy issues that govern the management of money in unmarried couples, the expectations that individuals bring into a couple are undeniably influenced by cultural gender role constructions. A great deal has been written about the traditional marriage with man as breadwinner and woman as bread maker. Although the feminist movement and women's increased participation in work outside the home have altered the rigidity of these roles, and the rigidity of the gender-role assumptions associated with them, most men and women still enter marriage with clear expectations that the man will be the major earner and the woman will have primary responsibility for the home and children. Despite sweeping social changes, the notion that the man should be older, taller, and richer than the woman is still commonly held.

In contrast, same-sex relationships have no such socially defined expectations, and gender-specific role assignments are up for grabs. Marcus (1998) thinks that this is a positive development as "the economic realm of the relationship can evolve organically" (p. 179). Although it is true that outside the legal dictates of conventional marriage things can evolve without the constraints of social expectations, there are unique challenges that go with entering into uncharted territory.

Moreover, although there are currently few, if any, social constructs governing same-sex marriages, the individuals in these partnerships have presumably assimilated not only the social constructs around money for their respective gender roles, but all of the expectations for how those constructs are acted out within the context of a relationship. When both partners enter the relationship with firmly rooted gender-role assumptions and expectations — even if these are unconscious or unacknowledged — the relationship will typically be somewhat skewed.

Gender skewing refers to a tendency in same-sex couples to drift toward the societal role expectations for their gender. Two men, for example, may have more difficulties around wage competition whereas two women may run into trouble around unspoken, unresolved expectations of being supported by the other partner. The presence and degree of gender skewing in a relationship depends on the life-cycle stages of the partners and to what extent they have internalized conventional gender role definitions. In addition, gender skewing may relate to how much money a couple has. Because men earn more than women, households with two working men will presumably earn more money than households with two working women or a heterosexual working couple. Regardless of their actual income, myths about gay earning and spending power can also affect the expectations brought into same-sex relationships.

The degree to which societal expectations determine how money is handled in a relationship varies. Many heterosexual couples, married and unmarried, keep their money separate despite conventional expectations that they conjoin. Many gay and lesbian couples, on the other hand, move toward a union of their finances as a way of demonstrating commitment. Ultimately, however, the ways in which a couple, same sex or heterosexual, navigates the shared financial realm depends primarily on the individual characters of the two people involved and the quality of intimacy in the relationship.

Money Can't Buy Me Love
In Amy Tan's (1989) *The Joy Luck Club*, a young married woman, Lena St. Clair, nervously anticipates an impending visit from her Chinese mother. Lena knows that her mother will see that something is wrong in her daughter's marriage. She will learn this because she will see that there is no sharing in the relationship. The couple keeps rigid accounts of each penny spent so that they can reimburse each other for items not jointly used, or for purchases not mutually desired. Interestingly, the couple developed this elaborate accounting system for tracking household expenses so that Lena would not be perceived as dependent or wanting to be taken care of. This focus on keeping things "even," however, ironically throws the relationship completely out of balance and causes it to fall apart. Here, Tan shows how money issues and a married couple's inability to solve them are indicative of deeper issues involving intimacy and commitment.

During sessions with Ellen, I found myself thinking of the story of Lena St. Clair, which I shared with her. Ellen was referred to me after her breakup with Mary, a woman with whom she had been involved for more than 10 years. The two had raised Mary's son Robert together. The boy's father had died of a rare cancer when Robert was a toddler, several years before Ellen and Mary met. Robert was now away at college, and Ellen reported that her relationship with Mary started to unravel when the teenager left and came to an end when it was discovered that Ellen had been involved with another woman. Mary was alternately enraged and despondent over the betrayal. Ellen's solution was to offer Mary a financial settlement that would provide for Robert's education.

Ellen was not completely without remorse, and she came to treatment to gain a better understanding of herself and of what had gone wrong with Mary. At the same time, she began a new, long-distance relationship with Linda, which continued in spite of many disagreements, particularly about money. Ellen reported that one of the reasons she was initially attracted to Linda was her financial independence. Linda was also professionally successful and lived in a large Midwestern city. An early struggle between the two had been over whether one or the other would relocate so that they could live together. It was ultimately Ellen who prevailed and Linda moved to New York.

Although Ellen described being drawn to Linda because she wanted "a partnership with an equal," she tried to exert financial control with Linda in the same way that she had with Mary. With Mary, Ellen asserted her right to make financial decisions because she was the earner. With Linda, an ongoing power struggle developed that was characterized by an informal and sometimes unconscious accounting system that was almost as dramatic as the one used by Lena St. Clair and her husband.

In the stormy relationship between Ellen and Linda, money concerns were paramount. Whereas Ellen spent money easily on luxury items, she chose for her partner a woman who prided herself on simplicity and practicality, so the couple would disagree about virtually every purchase, from a coffeepot to a pet. Linda wanted to adopt a pet from a shelter, while Ellen spent countless hours communicating with breeders and searching for the perfect purebred dog. These repeated arguments kept Ellen and Linda at a distance, which left Ellen feeling misunderstood and isolated — her greatest fear.

For Ellen, early issues of abandonment made it difficult for her to trust and share, and having a lot of money in the bank served as a talisman against her fear of being alone in the world. Whenever she put her faith in Linda as a safe harbor, she became frightened of her dependency and feared that Linda would take advantage of it and try to control her. It appeared that both women wanted to be taken care of and were constantly testing to see if the other would come through.

While Ellen took many steps forward and backward on her road to union with Linda, fear prevailed. Money, and conflicts about how to spend it, seemed to be the surest way to keep her neediness and desire for Linda out of her awareness, and she remained secure in her insecurity. In this relationship, money arguments served to maintain a level of separation that appeared to keep things safe. Like Lena St. Clair, Ellen was afraid to allow herself to feel dependent on her partner and lost the chance for the genuine intimacy that may have come from fully allowing herself to succumb to the relationship.

Looking for Ozzie and Harriet

Mike and Peter illustrate the collision between values of the dominant heterosexual culture and the less clearly defined values and partner role expectations of a gay male subculture. Referred by his cardiologist after Mike's hospitalization for coronary surgery, the two men, both in their 50s, had been involved for close to 30 years. They did not live together, however, and had always been nonmonogamous. Nevertheless, Mike considered Peter to be his "husband," and, in that role, Peter came to the hospital for family group sessions focusing on Mike's postoperative life. It was suggested by the group leader that Mike and Peter begin therapy together after Mike's discharge.

The two men were strikingly different in their presentations. Peter, somber, quiet, and somewhat passive, spoke of his concern for Mike and fears that he might have a heart attack and die. Other than that, Peter seemed complacent about the relationship. He expressed neither problems nor expectations.

Mike, on the other hand, complained openly about the state of their union. He seemed to long for a conventional marital situation and did everything he could to fit the "queer" peg of their relationship into the round hole of heterosexual matrimony. He longed for a shared apartment, regretted not having raised children, involved Peter in his extended family, resented his own exclusion from Peter's family, and tried in every possible way to provide financially for Peter. His will, retirement accounts, and insurance policies listed Peter as the beneficiary. He put Peter on his apartment lease and obtained domestic partner health insurance benefits for Peter through his employer. Peter, it seemed, contributed minimally to the relationship. The full weight of making a "marriage" of their relationship seemed to fall on Mike.

Peter's lack of ambition or goals was not limited to his relationship with Mike. He approached his career with a similar level of passivity, earning little money, and was unable to afford more than the studio apartment he had lived in since graduate school. Because each man had an apartment that was too small for two people, and they felt they could not afford one larger one, they continued to live separately. This arrangement seemed to suit them both well as they had long ago decided that their sexual incompatibilities made it necessary for them occasionally to seek partners outside of the relationship. Both Peter and Mike found this arrangement to be culturally acceptable and were comfortable with it.

During the couple's therapy, it became increasingly clear that a focus on money was being used as a way to keep them at a comfortable distance. It also became clear to both men that Mike preferred fantasies of a committed marriage to a real union. Despite his constant complaints that Peter was not giving enough of a commitment, Mike actually had a partner who suited his ambivalent needs. He acknowledged in treatment that his desire to replicate the kind of financial interdependency he associated with marriage was really an attempt to assuage his guilt about not being able to be interdependent and sexually monogamous. Ironically, it emerged that Mike, so determined to have a husband, was more sexually active outside the couple and the one who insisted on an "open" relationship.

The Diva and Her Assistant
In contrast to Mike and Peter, Kay and Dale, together over 15 years, were the picture of a traditional monogamous "marriage." They lived the conventional family life that Mike had once dreamed about. They owned an apartment, had a large network of friends, and shared many cultural interests. Both women worked hard in their respective careers, and each reported high levels of job satisfaction. Despite this harmonious structure, Kay and Dale's struggles demonstrate that unresolved — and unconscious — financial issues can disrupt even the most committed relationship.

Kay and Dale sought treatment together for what they described as their only complaint, a radical change in their sex life. Both reported that lovemaking had always been passionate and enjoyable, and they were proud that they did not seem to lose interest in each other sexually in ways that they thought to be "stereotypical for lesbians." Their sexual life was clearly an important part of their identity as a couple that both partners deeply missed. Both agreed that it was Dale who had seemingly lost her desire for sex. Dale described that she was uninterested and unresponsive, but didn't know why. She reported feeling the same toward Kay as she always had, except completely removed sexually.

Our sessions revealed that while Kay and Dale enjoyed a rich life together, they avoided dealing with disagreements and resentments. Over time, it became clear that communication between the two was not always open, and both had a problem dealing with anger. Dale was characteristically meek in the relationship, and Kay was set up to play the role of "bully." She was hurt and offended by the terminology, revealing the sensitive side of her character so long ago covered with a thick skin to help protect against cruel and physically abusive foster parents. Dale, used to a lifelong capitulation to a demanding, tyrannical father, had developed a passive-aggressive character and was shocked in the treatment to learn how much power she had in the relationship. She was uncomfortable with this and had trouble realizing that her "strike against management" had "shut down the factory."

Although the two envisioned themselves as partners, one was really treated as a "superstar" in the relationship and the other a handmaiden to the headliner. Dale deeply resented her lack of financial power, and it became clear that she was unconsciously "checking out" rather than confronting her dissatisfactions. She was a full partner in the management of the household and in assisting in Kay's public relations business, but she did not have equal access to funds or to decision making because of her lesser financial contribution to the joint account. Kay generally settled important matters and also decided on all vacations, nonessential expenditures, and was the initiator of sex.

I conceptualized Dale's sexual rejection of Kay as an attempt at overthrowing management. She had trouble tolerating the idea that she had so much power, but once she began to own it, she was freer to express her dissatisfactions directly to her partner. Kay was equally unhappy with her "chief executive bully" role and had not fully realized how much she controlled Dale with money. She began to understand that while she had always felt that she was being extremely generous with Dale, she spent money in the ways that made her feel best, not always on what her partner really wanted.

A poignant example of the financial power struggle between the two women surfaced when Dale bought an expensive wedding present for mutual friends. Kay was critical of the amount of money that Dale spent on the gift. When Kay realized that she felt on some level that it was not Dale's money to spend, she gained insight into how she had been controlling the relationship by controlling the purse strings and keeping her supposed "partner" in a second-class status. As the financial resentments between the two women began to clear, they were able to renegotiate other inequities in the relationship. Dale, feeling "more alive," agreed to be in charge of sex for a while. Without the pressure of rejection, and with a fuller understanding that despite her initiating sex and spending, she was not always meeting her partner's needs, Kay was able to give up some control in the service of a more equal partnership. The two left couples therapy with a clearer understanding of the role money played in their relationship and a renewed interest in their sexual life.

God Bless the Child that Got His Own
A less successful treatment highlights another aspect of the difficulties that money can play in same-sex relationships. Here,
covert gender-role assumptions established unspoken and unrealistic expectations between the partners. Connie and Lois also
typify how early individual histories of deprivation will be carried into a relationship and profoundly influence each partner's
ability to trust the other and negotiate differences. Unresolved
early needs for nurturing and love, present in each of these
women, inhibited the capacity to be unguarded and prevented
them from achieving closeness or intimacy.

Connie and Lois had expressed anger freely. In fact, among my
most vivid memories in practice was the need to take a walk
outside after my initial consultation with them because it had
felt as if the air had been sucked out of the room and replaced
with something toxic. It was a painful experience to witness
rage and sadness expressed to such a palpable degree.

The two women reported that they were seeking therapy for
"sex, money, and time issues." Connie was an architect with a
large firm. Lois worked for a distant cousin in his landscaping
business whenever extra help was needed. She enjoyed the out-
door nature of the work but did not like the sporadic income.
The dichotomous structure of this couple's relationship was
immediately apparent. Connie enjoyed a successful professional career, whereas Lois always had difficulty making a living.
The couple lived in an apartment that Connie had owned and
redesigned before they met.

Lois had asked me over the telephone about the fee, and stated that it might be a problem. During the consultation, money
issues were so explosive for this couple that they could not
agree on how to pay me. Connie, the more financially comfortable of the two, wanted to pay the fee herself. Lois, uneasy with
this, wanted to pay a fair portion based on her income. I asked
them how they could work this out between them to pay me one
fee but they were unable to find a solution. They wanted individual bills, each reflecting their share of the fee and each wrote
me a separate check every month. When they asked how long
our work together would take, I told them I would have a better idea when they were able to give me one check for the two

of them. Money was symbolic of all the ways this couple could not get together.

The relationship between Lois and Connie was both volatile and accusatory. While the two women claimed to be in love, they appeared to be consumed by competitiveness, resentment, and rage. Lois complained bitterly of all the ways that Connie had failed her. Despite her wish for independence and reluctance to accept financial help from Connie, Lois wanted to be taken care of. Connie, generally silent and less explosive in the sessions, expressed exasperation about her seeming inability to satisfy her partner on any level.

Another difficulty was Connie's background of Orthodox Judaism. She struggled for years reconciling her homosexuality and her religious beliefs and had been married for a short time after college. She had given up Jewish orthodoxy before meeting Lois. Despite her protests to the contrary, she seemed disturbed by Lois's Catholicism. Both women felt rejected by their families and claimed to have no social support for their relationship. They had different ideas of how to spend time and few interests and friends in common. Lois seemed jealous of Connie's professional success and financial security, and Connie reported being jealous of a coworker with whom she believed Lois to be infatuated, despite Lois's denial. There were many serious issues in this relationship, but the treatment is being recalled here because those that came to the forefront centered on money.

Lois appeared demanding and petulant in the sessions. She was intractable in her belief that Connie was failing to meet her needs. Connie continued to be unaware of how she was failing. In the sessions, Connie displayed the lack of understanding of which Lois constantly accused her, but it remained unclear exactly what she did not understand. Connie's passivity and outwardly calm demeanor in the face of Lois's tirades only resulted in Lois "upping" the volume.

Lois continued to feel that she was not being heard and her needs were not being met. She was alternately furious and solicitous with me, vacillating between accusing me of being just like Connie and then leaving lengthy apologetic messages about how helpful the sessions were and how badly she felt about her behavior during them. What emerged was Lois's belief that

Connie should take better care of her monetarily. There was a
wish for material support and security, coupled with a belief
that Connie could provide it. Despite her expressed wish to pay
her own way for therapy and other joint bills, Lois was resentful of what she perceived as Connie's options due to her greater
income. Connie, who had accepted her partner's demands for
independence at face value, could not grasp that Lois's urgent-
ly expressed needs went well beyond money, nor did she have
the emotional capacity to give what Lois was demanding. After
a few months in treatment, Lois announced that she wanted to
end the relationship. The remaining sessions focused on trying
to facilitate a somewhat amicable breakup. Lois did wind up
accepting financial help from Connie to get her own apartment
and to pay for some courses she was taking. Lois had originally moved in with Connie when they decided to live together and
was alternately pleased with and scornful of her partner's
upper-middle-class lifestyle. When she decided to move out,
she demanded accommodations similar to those to which she
had begrudgingly become accustomed. Ironically, Lois had
grown up in upper-middle-class surroundings and had rejected
her parent's "bourgeois values" and lifestyle comforts. Her
ambivalence about money, which was clearly present before the
start of the relationship, found a strong voice during her relationship with Connie.

Connie, who had come from a relatively low-income background, was not insensitive to issues of deprivation and long-
ing, but she was not in conflict about having and not wanting.
She had worked hard for her material success and was willing
to share it with her partner. But, in the process, she seemed to
have walled off her emotional self to protect against feelings of
being unacceptable or left out. Lois's more obviously charged
feelings about money, along with her extreme neediness, kept
her in a struggle with herself and her partner. She seemed most
comfortable on the outside looking in the bakery window, but
was enraged at not having the bread.

In this case, individual psychologies dominated the interpersonal field in a way that would have been identical had the partners been in a heterosexual relationship. For Connie and Lois,
there was no getting outside of their own histories and their

own ways of being in a relationship with another person. The issue was not money. Rather, these partners could not share, collaborate, or make joint decisions. In this relationship, Lois and Connie acted out their complex individual histories of deprivation by becoming paralyzed around money issues.

One Has Money, the Other Doesn't
Two men in their 20s, together since college, exemplify a number of issues about how couples deal with money in general, but also serve to illustrate how the presence of individual wealth can affect a same-sex relationship. The consequences of the inability to marry and legally redistribute the wealth, coupled with the internalized questions of who should be the "breadwinner" in a gay male relationship, posed interesting challenges in this case.

When Hal entered individual treatment with me, he was in his early 20s and already in a deeply committed monogamous relationship with Evan. They considered themselves married, had commingled funds, and were planning a future that included having a family. Both men were in graduate school preparing for different, although related careers. The two met through a summer internship program when they were quite young. Although they were pursuing similar professions, their economic circumstances were vastly different. Hal came from a working-class family and had always supported himself through school with side jobs and scholarships. He attended an Ivy League college and planned on taking out student loans to pay for his graduate education. He was the most upwardly mobile member of his family and expected someday to earn enough to live a life of relative middle-class comfort. Hal described his partner as coming from a background of wealth and privilege. Evan had a trust fund from his grandparents, giving him financial autonomy that would only increase with the passage of time. He was comfortable in a moneyed world and had a sense of infinite possibilities. Although, like Hal, Evan was ambitious for career success, his goals did not appear to be financially driven. When the two met and fell in love, it became clear to Hal that he felt somewhat confused about money in the relationship. He didn't have any, and he knew how to handle that. Suddenly, however, the moments of his life were filled with expensive places and things. Evan made plans for both of them, picked up the check wherever they went, and bought lavish gifts for Hal. After graduation, Evan asked him to live together in an apartment that Hal would never have been able to afford on his own.

During treatment, Hal recalled early issues around money with his feeling that, with Evan, he really never knew where he stood or how much money he had to spend. Although Evan was enormously generous — his money issues seemed to revolve around a need to give it away — Hal felt he could never assume that he had any autonomy in terms of making decisions that involved spending money. He would accept the gifts that Evan gave, but did not always have money for what he needed. As he put it, "I could have used some underwear and not another cashmere sweater." Hal felt uncomfortable having so many things he could not afford and about not being able to voice his desires. He believed that he would be seen as asking for money if he expressed an interest in seeing a particular concert or buying something for their shared apartment.

Moreover, because Hal had not yet "come out" to his family, he had no way of explaining why his roommate would pay all the rent. How could he explain living in such a great apartment? He dreaded visits from people from his West Coast hometown. In treatment, Hal referred to his "double coming out" as his sudden wealth was only explicable in terms of his having "married" someone rich. Having grown up unaccustomed to wealth, Hal was observant about the impact it had on his life and the way he felt about himself as a person with access to money. He became aware of the fact that people treated him differently and that his affluence made others uncomfortable at times. He also referred to "coming out" about having money as an issue that was separate from his gay relationship.

At the time Hal entered treatment, he had become accustomed to living on Evan's trust fund. His internal conflicts, however, were hardly resolved. He reported no difficulty paying for multiple analytic sessions each week and stated that the two now had a joint account to which he had complete access. Although Hal's issues about the ambiguity of day-to-day spending had lessened, his feelings about them remained intense.

There were also issues about his male identity and his strong feelings that it was somehow wrong to be supported by another man. As an educated, professional man he felt insulted by the stereotype of "boy toys," young gay men who seek out the company of richer partners and feared being viewed in this disparaging manner.

Hal identified his concerns in individual treatment and began to recognize his part in perpetuating his sense of being the "junior partner." He began to communicate these feelings more articulately to Evan and reported that, for the first time, he was able to make Evan understand what it felt like to be Hal in the relationship. Consequently, Hal became increasingly comfortable sharing in the wealth. Evan remained committed to finding ways to empower Hal in the relationship and help him to feel equal. Some of these efforts would prove to be difficult in the face of legal constraints, but Hal and Evan both worked on instilling a feeling of ownership in Hal that was separate from financial ownership. Things also improved when Hal began working and earning a regular paycheck from his position in a large firm where he feels he has a strong future.

The sense of personal security that each of these men has, along with their genuine love for each other and commitment to a life together, have helped them negotiate this difficult terrain. Their relative youth when they decided to live together also contributed to the ease with which they were able to blend their lives and make them one. Unfortunately, the fact that they are not permitted to marry legally serves to reinforce the essential fact that most of the money the two live on belongs to Evan and not to the couple. The reminders of this fact occasionally evokes old sensitivities in Hal, but he and Evan are constantly finding new and better ways to overcome them.

Conclusion

Money, like sex, is an important issue in relationships. The way people deal with money reflects a great deal about their characters, their histories, and the influences of the cultures and subcultures in which they live. In addition, as the above case material here illustrates, financial problems often mask other problems in a relationship, although money in and of itself can be the problem. Different styles of dealing with money can polarize a couple in much the same way as other differences, causing each to take an extreme position that is often experienced as irreconcilable.

Conventional wisdom suggests that the less money people have, the more they fight about it. My own clinical observations do not support that view. People have different ideas about how much money is enough and vastly different ideas about handling finances in the context of the couple. With the exception of relationships that are extremely stressed because there is not enough money to pay for basic needs, money issues will be governed by who the people are and not how much they have. For those willing to take a chance on love, there seems to be a concomitant willingness to take a chance on money. While same-sex pairs may have some additional external barriers to inhibit union, individuals in pursuit of real intimacy will find it and also will find ways to overcome obstacles.

Relationships in which partners are willing to share themselves are those in which money can be shared and differences in spending styles resolved. Open communication and willingness to risk intimacy make the simple math of one plus one come out even.

References

Lieberman, A. & Lindner, V. (1987), *Unbalanced Accounts: Why Women Are Still Afraid of Money*. New York: Atlantic Monthly Press.

Liss-Levinson, N. (1990), Money matters and the woman analyst: In a different voice. *Psychoanal. Psychol.*, 7 (Suppl.):119–130.

Marcus, E. (1998), *Together Forever*. New York: Anchor Books.

Mellan, O. (1992), Money polarities in couples. *Family Ther. Networker*, 16(2):47.

Merkin, D. (1999), Our money, ourselves. *The New Yorker*, April 26/ May 3, pp. 88–104.

Tan, A. (1989), *The Joy Luck Club*. New York: Putnam.

Index